Rev. Francis R. Davis
Our Lady Of Lourdes
120 Fairmont Road
Elmira, N. Y. 14905

THE MYSTERY OF SALVATION

PAUL DE SURGY

The Mystery
of Salvation

Translated by Rosemary Sheed

UNIVERSITY OF NOTRE DAME PRESS

NIHIL OBSTAT: JOANNES COVENTRY, S.J.
   CENSOR DEPUTATUS

IMPRIMATUR: ✠ PATRITIUS CASEY, VIC. GEN.

WESTMONASTERII, DIE 2A FEBRUARII 1966

The *Nihil Obstat* and *Imprimatur* are a declaration that a book or pamphlet is considered to be free from doctrinal or moral error. It is not implied that those who have granted the *Nihil Obstat* and *Imprimatur* agree with the contents, opinions or statements expressed.

FIRST AMERICAN EDITION 1966
UNIVERSITY OF NOTRE DAME PRESS
NOTRE DAME, INDIANA
Library of Congress Catalog Number: 66-21167

FIRST PUBLISHED 1966
SHEED AND WARD LTD
LONDON

© ROSEMARY SHEED, 1966

Originally published as *Les grandes étapes du mystère du salut*, Les Editions Ouvrières, Paris 1958.

Printed in Great Britain

Contents

Foreword ix

1. IS THERE A "MYSTIQUE" IN THE BIBLE? 1
   What a "mystique" is 1
   The Old Testament: a mystique based on promises 3
   The New Testament: a mystique in the full sense 4
   The Pauline presentation 5
   Special characteristics 8
   The major stages in the mystery of salvation 9
   Using this book 9

2. CREATION AND SIN 11
   The beginnings 11
   What should we look for in them? 12
   The creation accounts 14
   The cosmogony—first account 14
   The second account: creation and the fall 17
   The uniqueness of the first pair 21
   Creation and the Christian mystique 25

3. ABRAHAM, FATHER OF THE CHOSEN PEOPLE 27
   Abraham's importance in the bible 27
   Abraham, a man in history 28
   The Genesis accounts 30
   The calling of Abraham 32
   The promise 34

Attitudes of God and man	35
Abraham, God's friend	37
Abraham and ourselves	38

4. PLACES AND DATES IN BIBLE HISTORY 40
   - Bible lands — 40
   - Palestine, centre of the "fertile crescent" — 43
   - The bible and the history of the ancient east — 45
   - The great dates in bible history — 47

5. MOSES AND THE EXODUS 53
   - The Hebrews in the land of Egypt — 53
   - Moses — 54
   - The exodus and history — 56
   - The departure from Egypt — 60
   - The God of the exodus — 64
   - The exodus elsewhere in the bible — 65

6. MOSES AND THE COVENANT 68
   - The covenant of Sinai and the destiny of Israel — 68
   - The covenant at Sinai — 69
   - The God of the covenant — 70
   - The object of the covenant — 72
   - The rites concluding the covenant — 74
   - The covenant of Sinai, prelude to the new covenant — 76
   - The covenant of Sinai and the Christian people — 77

7. PROPHECY AND THE PROPHETS 79
   - Religious and political framework — 79
   - Prophecy as a major element in Israel's religious life — 80
   - The prophets mentioned in the bible — 82
   - What a prophet was — 85
   - The unique role of the prophets in Israel — 89
   - Some types of prophet — 91
   - Christians and the prophets of Israel — 97

8. THE EXILE   100
    The exile in Babylonia   100
    Factors in the renewal   102
    Israel's religious guides   103
    The exile in Israel's religious history   111
    The exile has a lesson for Christians   113

9. THE SAGES OF ISRAEL   115
    The sages of the ancient east   115
    The sages in Israel   118
    The Israelite sage   119
    The writings of the sages   123
    The sages' role   129

10. THE POOR OF YAHWEH   132
    Pitfalls to avoid   132
    The vocabulary of poverty   134
    The spirituality of the poor in the movement of history   135
    The poor of Yahweh   144
    Mary, high point of the hope of the poor   147
    Christ, the poor man of God   148
    The relevance of the lesson of the poor   148

11. CHRIST   151
    Christ in continuity with the history of salvation   151
    Jesus at the centre of the plan of salvation   153
    The person of Jesus   154
    The three phases of the mystery of Jesus   157
    Christ, source of grace and truth   163
    The new commandment   165
    Our attitude towards Christ   167

12. THE CHURCH   169
    The church in the continuity of salvation history   169
    Christ and the church   172
    The Spirit and the church   175

The church's mission	179
Aspects of the church	184
The attitude of the Christian in the church	187

13. THE SALVATION OF JEWS AND PAGANS — 190
The problems	190
The principles	192
The salvation of the non-evangelised	195
The salvation of the Jews	199
Christian attitudes	205

14. THE RETURN OF CHRIST — 209
Faith in Christ's return	209
Vocabulary and literary form	211
The parousia	214
The completion of the history of salvation	218
When the parousia will be	221
The Christian in expectation of the parousia	224

15. THE BIBLE, LIGHT OF OUR LIFE — 227
Revelation of God as directing the history of salvation	227
A mystique of worldwide dimensions	229
Showing the meaning of world history	230
Casting light on the present situation of Christians	232
Showing Christians their role in God's plan	236
The Christian attitude to the revelation of salvation	237

Bibliography	241
Maps Palestine	42
The "Fertile Crescent"	44
Table Great dates in bible history	48–52

Foreword

This book is the result of two occurrences.

A few years ago, at the end of a talk I was giving on the covenant to priests involved in parish work, I apologised for having said so little that could be of any relevance to their pastoral preoccupations. A regional chaplain of the YCW said that, on the contrary, he had noticed that an awareness of the great sweep of bible history gave his young Christian workers, who lived among young people enthralled with a mystique of the masses, a sense of being equal in that they, too, have a mystique of worldwide scope. This struck me as a most important observation.

The second thing dates from a Congress of Catholic Institutes that took place in Angers in 1955: as often happens at such meetings, professors and students were all asking one another how the Catholic Institutes could help those who attended them to acquire a synthesis of Christian thought, and on this occasion we began discussing the meaning of history. Following upon that, the biblical courses for the winter of 1955–6 were on the subject of the major stages in the mystery of salvation. At each session, when the theme had been developed, it was worked out by a team of students—among whom I should like especially to thank Jean-Yves Hameline and Jean-Marie Chupin (theology), Yann Page (law), Marie-Madeleine Humeau (science) and Anne de Ferrière (education). The faithfulness of the students in attending, and their wish (coupled with the encouragement of Père Gerfaud and M. Gelin) that I publish the talks, led me to decide to do so.

I need hardly say that this book makes no pretence to originality: it makes use of the common fund of exegetical knowledge, and the reader will often be referred to serious works of popularisation—of which there are so many today. This book is one of many that have resulted from an experience of using the bible in pastoral work, and it has been written in order to help lay people to make a beginning with scripture by giving them as a starting point a total view of the mystery of salvation, and getting them, from the first, to look for the word of life in the bible. It may also help some readers who are already familiar with the bible to see its unity better, and be of assistance to priests in preparing work with study groups.

The subject is so vast that each stage in the mystery of salvation can only be treated in a schematic way here. This makes it possible to get a better grasp of the major outlines of God's plan, but does not obviate the need for a deeper knowledge—especially with regard to the chapters on Christ, the church, and the salvation of those to whom the gospel has not been preached. For the same reason this book must not be expected to solve such complex problems as the literary form of the beginning of Genesis, the historicity of the plagues of Egypt, or the character of the traditions in the Pentateuch. I have simply sketched out certain lines of solution in order to prevent the reader's being brought up short by objections, and enable him to read further and find more detailed explanations in the works of specialists. Similarly, the applications to Christian living that follow the various sections are only outlines, and call for a lot of filling in.

The notes upon which this book is based were designed for oral teaching; I hope I have given references to all the books I have made use of, and ask to be forgiven if through error I have omitted any.

If, despite all its imperfections, this book helps even one reader to make contact with the word of God, and understand more fully the vocation the Lord has marked out for him in the history of salvation, then it will have fully achieved its object.

PAUL DE SURGY

Angers, 18 March, 1958

1

Is there a "mystique" in the bible?

What a "mystique" is

Do we find a mystique in the bible, God's message to men?

Before we can answer this question, we must decide precisely what it means. First of all there is a distinction between a mystique and mysticism. When we speak of mystical theology, or of people who are mystics, we are referring to the spiritual relations between the soul and God, particularly in their loftier heights; we speak of mystical states and ways, of great mystics like St Bernard, St John of the Cross or St Thérèse of Lisieux.... One has only to open the bible, which is first and foremost a religious book, to see that it contains a doctrine of the spiritual life; think of the mystical accents of Jeremiah, the psalmists and St Paul, the contemplative elements in St John! Yet this is not really an answer to the question asked above. For in our day we use "mystique" to mean something rather different; when we say someone has a mystique, we mean that he is filled with an ideal by which he acts, and which upholds him in all he undertakes. Thus one can speak of the Nazi mystique, meaning the ideology based on the principle of domination by a racial group, which moved its adherents to try to bring about that domination; we also generally speak of the Marxist mystique, meaning a materialist view of the world and its evolution which inspires real, if misdirected, devotion; and finally, we talk of the Christian mystique, meaning a view of the world and its destiny inspired by faith and translated into life. If we know what to look for, we can see the effects of this Christian mystique every day; it alone can explain the martyr dying for Christ, the missionary or nun who gives up everything to preach the gospel, the priest who renounces the human promise of a family to be more fully at the service of God and his fellow men, the Catholic Actionist who sometimes refuses the promotion due him in order to remain closer to his brothers, the layman who bears witness to Christ in his family and society.

Thus it would seem that a mystique can be defined as "a vision of the world and of history which inspires a man to act and gives direction to his action". It has three characteristics: its universal scope, its dynamism, and its repercussion on living. A mystique provides a *vision of the world* which enables everyone to be aware of his place in the universe and his solidarity with mankind as a whole; in this it provides something like the support a scientist finds in his laboratory or a worker in his factory—the fact of knowing that one's work has its place and usefulness in the world. A mystique includes a *vision of history*, of the world as being on the move: this dynamic view of things and events helps man to recognise the contribution he can make to the development of history and the future of the world, both materially and spiritually. And lastly, a mystique is a vision which inspires and directs action: the man with a mystique is, by definition, active.[1] Where there is a vision of the world and of history that does not affect the life and action of its possessor, then it can be called a theory, an opinion, a point of view perhaps, but not a mystique.

So, having defined the word, can we say that the bible contains a mystique?

The answer must surely be that it does.

The Old Testament: a mystique based on promises

Even in the Old Testament the elements of a mystique are present. Abraham set off for an unknown land, strong in God's promise of a blessing that should extend from him to all the nations of the earth. (Gn 13 : 1–4.) The unweary-

[1] With a Christian, it is not simply a question of being active. Congar rightly observes, "An apostle is a man of God, not merely a propagandist. He is a living element in God's plan of salvation, an emanation, as it were, of Christ himself..." [*The Mystery of the Church*, London 1960, 44–5.]

ing activity of the prophets, champions of God's cause, was rooted in faith that Yahweh, the master of history, was guiding events towards the goal he had fixed.[1] The Israelites retained faith and hope in Yahweh because they were aware of belonging to a people who were the bearers of God's promise: "For he is our God, and we are the people of his pasture, and the sheep of his hand." (Ps 95 : 7.) And there were also the righteous, whose hopes lay in immortality, and whose conduct was contrasted by the sage with that of the impious who did not know the secret plans of God or the immortal destiny he intended for man.

However the mystique of the Old Testament is essentially a mystique based upon promises whose fulfilment is still in the future.

The New Testament: a mystique in the full sense

With the New Testament, the bible produces a mystique in the full sense of the term: Christ is come, has fulfilled the promise, founded the church, and promised to return. In him God's plan of salvation is revealed and realised, and the bible offers all men a vision of the world and of history that can inspire them to action, and direct their activity. This mystique is revealed on every page of the New Testament. Indeed it

[1] See Chapter 7, "Prophecy and the prophets", below, pp. 79–99.

is the proclamation, made by Peter at Pentecost, of the salvation of the world in Jesus, dead and risen again, and accompanied by an invitation to enter into it. (Ac 2 : 14–40.) It is the prologue to John's gospel, announcing the arrival of the eternal Word among men, and the divine sonship he brings to all who believe in him. (Jn 1 : 1–18.) It is the cosmic vision of redemption in Christ given by St Paul in Ephesians. (1 : 2–10; Col 1 : 18–20.) And it is also the message in the Book of Revelation to the persecuted Christians, assuring them of God's final victory, and helping them to hold firm, directing their minds to the heavenly Jerusalem and Christ's coming in glory. Such a vision of the world and of history is certainly a mystique, for it gives direction to the Christian's activity, and inspires him to expend himself for Christ; it brings with it a call to conversion, sustains the perseverance of the persecuted, and requires the cooperation of human beings—this is faith in the Johannine sense.

The Pauline presentation

Three complementary expressions that St Paul uses to speak of the plan of salvation will help us grasp the essential character of the Christian mystique: the counsel of God (the Jerusalem Bible gives "le dessein de Dieu"), the wisdom of God, and the mystery.

In his farewell speech to the elders of Ephesus, Paul cried: "Therefore I testify to you this day that I am innocent of the blood of all of you, for I did not shrink from declaring to you the whole counsel of God." (Ac 20 : 26–7.) That "counsel" is none other than the plan of salvation conceived by God from all eternity and fulfilled in Christ Jesus: St Paul speaks of it at length in the epistle to the Ephesians, where he talks of "the eternal purpose which he has realised in Christ Jesus our Lord". (3 : 11.) The knowledge of that purpose gives the Christian his own special vision of history.

The "wisdom of God" in St Paul always refers to God's eternal salvific idea of the world being saved in Christ.[1] The wisdom of God does not follow the same laws as the wisdom of the world, and is actually opposed to it in so far as it refuses God. The wisdom of God reaches its goal through the mystery of the cross, and it is revealed in Christ crucified: "He it is who, by being given to the world, makes available to us a profound knowledge of the wisdom of God."[2] The believer, by adhering to Christ and his message, has access to that wisdom, and gains along with it his own special yardstick for appreciating things and events.

There are many places where St Paul speaks of the mystery he is called to announce. (Rom 16 : 25–6; Eph 3 : 3–10.) This is the mystery "which was not made known to the sons of men

[1] See L. Cerfaux, *Christ in the Theology of St Paul*, Edinburgh and London 1959.
[2] Cerfaux, 206.

in other generations", but "hidden for ages in God", and is now "revealed to his holy apostles and prophets by the Spirit": its object is simply the announcing of salvation in Christ and the proclaiming of his message—hence it is "the mystery of Christ". (Eph 3 : 4.) The revelation of this mystery gives the Christian a special mystique all his own.

What is proclaimed in the New Testament, then, is the eternal plan of salvation that God has for the world and which centres upon Christ, the revelation of divine wisdom made known in Christ crucified and achieved in ways that are baffling to the wisdom of "the world", and the manifestation of the mystery which has been hidden in God from the beginning of time, and prepared for our glory, whose object is the realisation of salvation in Christ: "But we impart a secret and hidden wisdom of God, which God decreed before the ages for our glorification. None of the rulers of this age understood this; for if they had, they would not have crucified the Lord of glory. But, as it is written, 'No eye has seen, nor ear heard, nor the heart of man conceived, what God has prepared for those who love him.'" (1 Cor 2 : 7–9.)

To know God's counsel, God's wisdom and his mystery—in other words to know the mystery of salvation—imparts a vision of the world and of history peculiar to the bible which reveals it, and it is that which constitutes the Christian mystique.

Special characteristics

The whole of this book is about the mystery of salvation, but it is worth while here to point out some of the elements that characterise it. We note as we leaf through the bible that God's plan is fulfilled progressively, that it is a question of gradual revelation, of morally educating the people of God, of salvation in different historic stages. The biblical conception of time is not a cyclical one, based on the periodic renewal of events, as with the Greeks, but a linear one, made up of a succession of once-and-for-all actions directed towards the final goal of history.[1] The accomplishment of salvation at once presents both a personal and a community aspect; the man of the bible is neither an isolated individual, nor a faceless member of a group, but a person who belongs to a people. The Christian mystique is cosmic in scope, for it gives a vision of the world, and is eternal in its dimensions; it does not drag the Christian away from this world's work, but sees eternal repercussions from everything he does. The centre of both the revelation and the fulfilment of the plan of salvation is Christ. And Christian history is directed towards its completion which will happen at the end of time with the return of Christ.

[1] See Jean Daniélou, *The Lord of History*, London 1958, 1–3.

The major stages in the mystery of salvation

Several factors explain the plan followed for studying the mystery of salvation. The first is to indicate the general framework of the divine plan, and the major stages of history: the creation, the election of Abraham, the exodus, the covenant, the exile,[1] the redeeming incarnation, the church, the coming of the Lord. I have also sought to spotlight the different people who were important in the unfolding of salvation: Abraham, Moses, the prophets, the sages, the poor of Yahweh, Christ, the church. In dealing with the history of salvation, it is also necessary to consider—at least summarily—the problem of Israel and the Gentiles. And finally, it has seemed useful in conclusion to bring together the different points of view about God and man's attitude to him that have emerged from all that has been said.

Using this book

I cannot too strongly urge those who use this book as a first guide to the bible to read the corresponding passages from the bible, indicated after each chapter. But to receive the word of

[1] Every choice involves limitations; for the Old Testament I have kept what seems most important from the point of view of the history of the people of God and the point of view of pinpointing the mystique of the bible, but these first glimpses should be filled in as soon as possible by a study of the period of the kings, of Judaism and the development of messianism under the old law.

God mere reading is not enough; one must be able to pray with the bible, receiving it with faith in the Christian assembly, or silently meditating the Christian text by oneself. And further, to hear the word of God sincerely, we must want to bring our lives into accord with the mystique it reveals; the lines of thought suggested at the end of each chapter are no substitute for personal and practical effort.

Reading the bible, if it is undertaken in this spirit, cannot fail to awaken a longing for a deeper understanding of the divine message, and an ever more genuine personal response to God's plan of salvation for the world.

Reading

Eph 1 : 3–19, and 3 : 8–12

2

Creation and sin

The beginnings

Though the history of Abraham, which is the start of the formation of the chosen people, begins only with chapter 12 of Genesis, the bible begins by explaining the origins of the world and of mankind. There are two main reasons for these pages being included in sacred scripture.

Everyone who gives any thought to the problem of the meaning of life must ask the questions: How was the world created? Where do evil, suffering, sin and death come from? In simple and pictorial language, the first chapters of Genesis answer these questions, and reveal "the fundamental truths upon which the economy of salvation rests"[1]; they may therefore be called the blackcloth against which the history of salvation unfolds, and their place in the bible needs no explanation.

But, we must go further; with the revelation of the bible, as with the tradition of the church, the history of salvation begins not with the election of Abraham, but with the creation of the

[1] R. de Vaux, OP, *La Genèse*, Paris 1951, 35.

world. For as Daniélou notes, the creation "remains an historical event, itself the inauguration of the time-process, and as such belongs to the general history of salvation."[1] Thus the first chapters of Genesis are indispensable to any total revelation of God's plan.

What should we look for in them?

A superficial mind without great literary sensibility, finding the style of the creation accounts surprising, might be tempted to believe that they contain nothing of any value. They describe a world created in six days, whereas everyone knows that a very long time elapsed between the world's taking shape and the appearance of man. And what kind of transcendent God would shape man like a potter? Above all, what can be thought of a God so terrible as to deprive man of his friendship for disobeying him by eating some fruit? To be held back by objections of this kind indicates a total failure to understand the literary form of the first three chapters of Genesis by expecting their writers to express themselves like moderns. But God respects the men he is dealing with, and lets the sacred author speak according to the culture and language of his time; this should be remembered when we interpret the texts, though it in no way lessens their doctrinal importance.

On the other hand, we must not seek a scientific explanation of the internal constitu-

[1] Daniélou, 28.

tion of the world in these chapters: they will not reveal either the date of the creation, nor the succession of geological stages, nor any proof of evolution. Everything, indeed, indicates that the author has no intention of giving information of that kind; he is interested only in the underlying truths of a religious nature—that God created the world, that he intervened specially to create man and woman, and so on.

Nor do we find photographs or a record of attested facts—there was no equipment for producing such things in Eden. "The events concerned belong to a sphere beyond the furthest horizon of historical time; they cannot therefore be the object of any human testimony. The epoch to which they belong is ... so distant from us that we cannot admit the possibility of a tradition that might have preserved the memory of any details."[1]

What we must look for in these texts is the truths that the sacred author wished to teach, so we must differentiate between the writer's mode of expression and the doctrine expressed. Since some of those truths are events, we can be certain of them also—but we must of course distinguish between literary device, and the fact underlying it. Having made this distinction, however, it is perfectly legitimate to speak of the historical nature of the first chapters of Genesis,[2] and to try to ascertain its extent.

[1] A. Robert, "Genres littéraires de l'Ancien Testament", in *Initiation biblique*, 3rd ed., Paris 1954, 283.
[2] de Vaux, *La Genèse*, 35.

The creation accounts

The bible begins with two accounts of the creation (Gn 1: 1–2, 4, and Gn 2: 4 – 3: 24), the second being the older. At first sight this may seem strange, but it is really quite natural, for the accounts, far from repeating one another, are complementary, and their arrangement is completely logical. The first relates to the creation of the universe, whose summit is man, and the second to man's creation and destiny.

The cosmogony—first account

The first and more recent account (sixth century BC) describes, in majestic and almost liturgical style, the creation of the universe and man. It belongs to the "priestly" tradition,[1] and manifests its main characteristics: a preoccupation with theology and liturgy, a sober style, a logical and carefully arranged presentation.

The detailed list of creatures is typically Semitic; where a Greek would have been content to declare that God created the world, a Semite must enumerate the creatures it contains, the fishes, beasts, birds and so forth.[2] The logic and

[1] The first five books of the bible, still called the Pentateuch, are the result of the fusion of several previously separate traditions—Yahwist, Elohist, deuteronomist and priestly—and the priestly tradition flowed from the sacerdotal centres of Jerusalem. A good general study of this question can be found in B. Anderson, *The Living World of the Old Testament*, London 1958.

[2] We find the same enumeration in the Canticle of the three young men (Dn 3 : 51–90), and Ps 8.

clarity of the priestly code shows clearly in the listing of the creatures. It has often been pointed out that the works of creation are set forth in an order that moves from the general to the particular and from the less perfect to the more perfect, and can be divided into two groups:

Separation of the elements	*Decoration of the universe*
Light—darkness	Sun—moon—stars
Waters above—waters below	Fish—birds
Earth—sea—plants	Animals
	Man

The preoccupation with ritual appears in the framework set round the work of creation, the week of work ending in a day of rest; this literary device was meant to remind the Israelites that the sabbath rest was willed by God.

An attentive examination of the text makes it clear that the author was not intending to give scientific details about the creation of things, with his artificial framework of a week, with light being created before the sun, with the logical order in which the creations are placed, and so on. On the other hand, the theological purpose is clear, and it is the underlying teaching that we must grasp. We cannot exhaust the meaning of the text here, but only stress a few points.

The Creator is the one God, distinct from the world and anterior to it. Compared with the

Mesopotamian myths, the bible account stands out in the transcendence and purity of its monotheism: God does not come out of chaos like the gods of Babylon, and he is distinct from the universe he creates. The sun and moon, the Assyrians' gods Samas and Sin, are creatures of the one God; and though the Semitic peoples were very given to star-worship, the biblical writer makes it clear that the stars shining so brightly in the eastern sky are only created things.

God created the world with wisdom; everything was planned in order and harmony—the plants with their seeds, the animals able to reproduce, and all was arranged with a view to giving man dominion over the world.

God created the universe by his omnipotence. To make this clear the writer describes God creating things effortlessly, by his word alone: "God said ... and it was so."

The fact that God deliberated with himself before creating man, the account of that creation (1:27), and God's words to the man and woman, reveal important truths in concrete language, namely, the special intervention of God in forming the first man and woman,[1] the dignity of man set above all other creatures and made in the image and likeness of God, and God's will

---

[1] This special intervention of God, which includes among other things the direct creation of souls, by no means excludes the possibility of God's making use of matter already existing and alive.

with regard to society and the fruitfulness of marriage.

And, finally, it is evident from this first account that creation left God's hands as something good; one phrase keeps recurring as a kind of *leitmotiv*: "God saw that it was good", and is repeated finally in v. 31: "And God saw everything that he had made, and behold it was very good."

The second account: creation and the fall

The second, older account (tenth or eleventh century BC) belongs to the Yahwist tradition.[1] It deals primarily with the creation and destiny of man. Having described the formation of man and woman and their first state, it records the fall and its consequences, which mark man's present state and put him in the situation of needing to be saved. "The subject is treated with a seriousness, delicacy and gravity that make these pages the finest in Genesis."[2] There should be nothing surprising about the language and imagery the author uses: his intention was to make himself understood. The oriental imagery which makes the story so exquisite is intended to translate religious teaching in a way that all could grasp. It is up to us to preserve the teaching, without being dominated by the imagery.

We can divide the main teachings into four

[1] This tradition is named after the documents that embody it, in which God is always called Yahweh.
[2] de Vaux, 43 *n*.

groups, in this order: those dealing with man and woman, with the fall, with the consequences of sin and with the promise of salvation.

Man and woman

In order to teach that God created man and gave him life, the author, having observed that man disintegrates into dust after death, and must breathe to live, describes God forming the first man out of clay and breathing the breath of life into his nostrils.

Man's superiority to the animals and his role as leader are expressed in the verses in which he names the animals (20), and the woman (23). The dignity of the woman comes precisely from her being like man, and therefore of the same nature, and made for his sake; the image of her being taken from his side expresses the identity of nature between man and woman, and the fact that they are complementary. By this teaching, the author is proclaiming the dignity of woman in a world which did not always recognise it.

The divine origin of marriage, its unity, and its permanence are expressed in *vv.* 21-4, concluding with: "Therefore a man leaves his father and his mother and cleaves to his wife, and they become one flesh." Their original happiness is suggested by the image that means so much in that part of the world—that of flowing rivers. And, finally, the state of innocence in which the man and woman were created is expressed by the absence of carnal concupiscence: "And the man and his wife were both naked and were not ashamed." (2 : 25.)

The fall

The tempter is shown in the guise of a serpent, because that was an image often linked with the fertility cults, so widespread in the East, which attracted the lukewarm among the Israelites and drew them away from the worship of Yahweh.

The first sin is shown as a sin of pride in the form of serious disobedience to God. For the knowledge of good and evil means in effect "the power to decide what is good and evil for oneself, and to act accordingly".[1] According to the symbolism of the story, eating of the tree that gives that knowledge against God's command thus represents "a claim to moral autonomy whereby man rejects his creaturely status, and reverses the order established by God".[2] This spirit of revolt, which lies at the root of all sin, shows how serious this first sin was. To interpret it literally in terms of a tree and fruit is not only to misunderstand the literary form of the account, but leads to a real danger of the reader's minimising the importance of the sin.

The consequences of sin

The first effect of sin was that friendship with God came to an end: God, the writer tells us, drove man out of the garden of Eden. (3 : 23–4.)

[1] de Vaux, 45 n.
[2] de Vaux, 45 n.

Among other effects were death ("You are dust, and to dust you shall return"), the loss of the gift of integrity ("The eyes of both were opened and they knew that they were naked") —the awakening of concupiscence is noted because it is "the most expressive manifestation of the disorder brought into the harmony of creation by man's revolt"[1]—suffering: here, rather than declaring in the abstract that suffering flows from sin, the writer lists some sufferings he sees (woman giving birth in pain, being dominated by her husband, the difficulty of work for the man), and declares them to be the result of sin. Thus man's present painful state is linked with original sin. It is important here not to include work among the consequences of sin; before the fall man had to cultivate and keep the garden of Eden. It is only the toilsome element that results from sin: "In the sweat of your face you shall eat bread."

The promise of salvation

A gleam of hope comes, however, with the promise of salvation. In man's struggle with the devil, God declares that man will have the final victory: "The Lord God said to the serpent... I will put enmity between you and the woman, and between your seed and her seed; he shall bruise your head, and you shall bruise his heel."

This promise is called the *proto-evangelium* because it is the far-off announcement of the salvation that is to come. Later chapters will be

[1] de Vaux, 97 *n*.

concerned with the historical unfolding of its fulfilment.

The uniqueness of the first pair

The author of Genesis 2-3 presents Adam and Eve as *a* particular couple. One must therefore consider the problem of the uniqueness of the first pair, in other words, of monogenism.

One must first note that the question of how many couples the human race is descended from is approached quite differently by the scientist and the theologian, and its solution will not lie along the same paths for both. On the theological level, which is that of revealed truth, one is faced with the alternative of monogenism or polygenism. The question is simply: Did the human race originate from one couple or from several? And the theologian will seek an answer to this question, not in arguments taken from human science, but in the word of God; he will speak in the light of faith. Knowing that the God who has spoken to men is also the God who made all things, he is secure in the knowledge that there will never be any contradiction between the true affirmation of faith and the sure conclusions of science. At the scientific level, of observation and experiment, the problem posed is not quite the same. The dilemma is between monophyletism or polyphyletism—in other words **does** humanity belong to a single phylum, or several? has it one human founder or several? At such a distance, in fact, science can only be concerned with totalities, and that is why "the problem of monogenism in the strict sense of the word seems to elude science as such by its very nature".[1] To solve the problem as he sees it, the scientist proceeds by way of observation and experiment. He does not set out to provide proof of monogenism—nor does the theologian ask him to. There can be no conflict between them except in the hypothetical case of its being proved beyond doubt that modern man descends from several different first groups which share no common human antecedent. But, simply from the scientific point of view, it would seem very difficult *a priori* to be able to reach these two certainties. In the present state of research, in any case, this hypothesis is not verified—indeed, it would seem, on the contrary, that the results of paleontological work are favourable to monophyletism: "If the science of man can say nothing directly for or against monogenism (a single initial couple) it can on the other hand come out decisively, it seems, in favour of monophyletism (a single phylum)."[2] As Père Dubarle wrote recently: "everything seems to indicate that there is enough indetermination in what paleontology can tell us to be able to uphold, without any illogicality, the religious affirmation that there was a first single human pair".[3]

[1] Pierre Teilhard de Chardin, *The Phenomenon of Man*, London 1959, 186, *n.* 1.

[2] Teilhard de Chardin, 188, *n.* 1.

[3] D. Dubarle OP, "Evolution et évolutionnisme", in *Lumière et Vie*, 34, 88. The whole of this article is well worth reading.

Having said all this, how are we to resolve the dilemma—monogenism or polygenism?

If one takes chapters 2–3 of Genesis in isolation, it is possible to say, despite the general term used to designate man, that the author took Adam and Eve to be specific individuals, not collective beings. However this is not sufficient to settle the question finally, for it does not seem as though the writer had the question of polygenism in mind. We may say, therefore, that his text as we have it deals with a single pair, but that, apart from the tradition of the church which is the only infallible interpreter of the word of God, it is not a complete answer to the problem.

In reality, if we are to put the problem properly, we must not be content to take this text in isolation, but must see it in relation to all the biblical texts, which, taken together, present Adam as a specific individual (for instance, Rom 5: 12ff.), to the patristic commentaries in which Adam is also held to be a definite person, and, above all, to the documents of the magisterium, and especially the fifth session of the Council of Trent on original sin. It was in the light of all this that Pope Pius XII, in his encyclical *Humani generis*, gave the following warning: "Christians cannot lend their support to a theory which involves the existence, after Adam's time, of some earthly race of men, truly so called, who were not descended ultimately from him, or else supposes that Adam was the name given to some group of our primordial ancestors. It does not appear how such views can be reconciled with the doctrine of original sin, as this is guaranteed to us by scripture and tradition, and proposed to us by the church. Original sin is the result of a sin committed, in actual historical fact, by an individual man named Adam, and it is a quality native to all of us, only because it has been handed down by descent from him."

The scope of this document must be neither magnified nor diminished. It is not a dogmatic definition of monogenism, and it must be understood with all the nuances the Pope intended. But it cannot be reduced to the mere announcement of a theological opinion; it is an act of the church's ordinary magisterium, through which the pope as guardian of faith excludes polygenism in regard to the origin of mankind as we know it. The document shows that the pope wants to preserve substantially the affirmation of the uniqueness of the first human pair because of its connection with the doctrine of the personal character and the transmission of original sin; and it is this motive of faith recalled by the pope which commands the submission of the believer to this act of the magisterium. All this, as you see, leaves us in the situation I described earlier of the theologian's attitude to the problem of monogenism.

Without in any way expecting theological research to make any change in our object of faith, the believer can, however, legitimately hope that in this matter the deepening of theological understanding on the one hand, and the advance of scientific knowledge about man on the other, will make it possible to bring the theological affirmation we have been looking at into closer harmony with the facts known to science.

Creation and the Christian mystique

After reading the creation accounts, it is valuable to regroup some of the teachings which govern man's attitude to God and his fellow man, and which colour his vision of history.

God, unique and transcendent, who made heaven and earth, is the same God who chose Abraham, who was made flesh,[1] who now gives every man the possibility of being saved, and who, at the end of time, will raise the living and the dead. To realise this is to realise how close God is to us, and to make creation seem a less distant event.

Man was created in God's image, and he should remember this in all his dealings with his fellow man. The biblical mystique thus stands completely apart from any system of thought that would cheapen the dignity of the human person.

Creation, as a work of God's omnipotence, makes the whole universe and especially man radically dependent on the Creator. Man's spiritual attitude, therefore, must be marked by a sense of that total dependence.

[1] Remembering, however, that it was the Word alone who was made flesh (Jn 1 : 14).

I have already pointed out the optimistic attitude of revelation towards the created world: creation comes from God's hands as something good, and the institution of marriage is willed by the Creator. The revelation of the bible has nothing in common with those philosophies which hold matter to be evil, or see marriage as a concession to human weakness. But it is not an unclouded optimism; one has but to read the account of the fall to realise that.

By the fall man has been placed in a state of destitution as regards salvation; every man must realise his need to be saved, and his total inability to attain salvation by his own powers.

To grasp the whole breadth of these first chapters of the bible we must recognise their dynamic aspect and their place in the history of salvation. As we have said, creation is also the beginning of time, the setting on foot of the divine plan. It is "the first step in God's plan, which is to culminate only in the creation of new heavens and a new earth".[1]

Reading

Gen. 1:1 – 2:4; 2:4 – 3:24; Ps 8; 19:1–7; 54; Jb 38:1–30

[1] Daniélou, 28.

3

Abraham, father of the chosen people

Abraham's importance in the bible

One thing the reader of the bible must soon realise is the exceptional importance of Abraham. Even statistically, his is one of the names most often mentioned, but the way in which it is mentioned is more significant still. When he appears in Genesis, two things especially underline his importance: he has a genealogy, and God changes his name. When a biblical writer presents someone illustrious, he often indicates who his parents and perhaps his ancestors were: in Gn 11 : 10–26, we are given the genealogy of Abraham, just as Matthew and Luke give us the genealogy of Jesus. Similarly, when God names a man, or changes the name he already has, it is generally the sign of some exceptional mission. It was so with John the Baptist (Lk 1 : 13) whose name meant "Yahweh has given grace", and whose job was precisely that of announcing the Messiah to the world; it was so with Simon, whose name our Lord changed to Peter because of the place he was to fill in the church. (Mt 16 : 18.) And in Genesis, God says to Abraham: "No longer shall your name be Abram, but your name shall be Abraham, for I have made you the father of a multitude of nations." (Gn 17 : 5.) It is clear, then, from the genealogy and this change of name, that we are in the presence of someone exceptional.

In the New Testament Abraham also stands out. St Matthew opens his gospel with Christ's genealogy, beginning with Abraham: "The genealogy of Jesus Christ, the son of David, the son of Abraham. Abraham was the father of Isaac..." (Mt 1 : 1–2.) In the Benedictus, Zachary, John the Baptist's father, greets the dawning of the Messianic era in these words: "Blessed be the Lord God of Israel: for he has visited and redeemed his people... and remembers his holy covenant, the oath which he swore to our father Abraham to grant us." (Lk 1 : 68f.) Mary concludes the Magnificat with a similar idea: "My soul magnifies the Lord.... He has helped his servant Israel in remembrance of his mercy: as he spoke to our fathers, to Abraham and to his posterity for ever." (Lk 1 : 46ff.) And Jesus himself describes the Kingdom of God in terms of a feast in which Abraham and the prophets are taking part. (Lk 8 : 28.)

Throughout the bible, then, Abraham appears as someone outstanding, whom we must know in order to understand God's plan.

Abraham, a man in history

There are many people for whom Abraham is a distant and mysterious person lost in the mists of time—almost a mythical character. But God does not carry out his plan of salvation with imaginary people; Abraham is a concrete man whom we can place in history.

He arrived in the land of Canaan[1] around 1850 BC; he was a semi-nomad, the shepherd of a few flocks, who lived in a town where he made contact with a settled population and adopted some of their customs. His name is not an unknown one—it occurs in a nineteenth-century text. The town of Ur, in the Chaldees, where he lived, had been governed by three dynasties, and ruled over Lower Mesopotamia until it was taken by storm in 1940 BC. His family's departure from Ur fits into the general framework of migrations of peoples at the beginning of the second millennium. Abraham arrived in Canaan five thousand years after the building of the first town on the site of Jericho—in other words, there is easily a thousand years longer between its foundation and Abraham than between Abraham and ourselves. The great pyramids of Egypt (2723–2563 BC) were older for Abraham than Notre-Dame de Paris is for us. Abraham's life is thus well within recorded history, and it is worthwhile to remind ourselves that this man, so different from us in culture and way of life, had a heart and a soul and a psychology like ours.

The bible does not tell us what he looked like or give any other details that would satisfy our

[1] i.e., Palestine when it was inhabited by a Canaanite population.

curiosity; it tells us of his calling, of the promise God made to him, of the work he accomplished. But before we study the account of these things, it is wise to begin by considering the general style and nature of that account in order to avoid misunderstanding it.

The Genesis accounts

These accounts are rather like family archives.[1]

Having been first handed down by word of mouth in the tribes and as part of their religion, repeated with care from generation to generation, the memories of their great ancestor were finally put in writing and have thus come down to us.

One must avoid two possible errors about them. The first is to expect these accounts to be as precise and factual as a modern legal statement; anxiety for strict exactitude in every detail is something peculiar to modern history, and it would be unfair to expect it in the accounts of the patriarchs. The second mistake would be the opposite one, that of underestimating the value of these traditions. In our time, thanks to the development of printing, everything of value on the scientific level is put down in writing, and memory plays almost no part in the transmission of knowledge; therefore twentieth-century man rather tends to consider

[1] With this difference, that they are dealing with a family that grew into a nation and was involved in religious history.

anything transmitted orally as being without interest. Yet it would be a mistake to apply this modern value-judgement unconsciously to documents dating from a period when, owing to their conditions of civilisation, people verified things in a quite different way. In patriarchal times the memory was much more used than it is today, and traditions were transmitted in the form of recitations, easily remembered thanks to assonance, mnemonics, popular etymology, play on words, and so on. The object of these traditions made it important to preserve them with care, and though their character as popular recitations made it possible for imagination to embroider here and there on the reality, the substance of what they recounted was well attested.

And, in fact, a certain amount of cross-checking leads us to realise that their content should not be discounted groundlessly. If we follow the journeyings of Abraham and the patriarchs, who were shepherds, on the map, we can see that they are in accord both with the rainfall map and with the political situation in the country, at that time occupied by the Canaanites.[1] At the period when these traditions were being put into writing, the people were no longer nomads, and political conditions were different; so, clearly, the patriarchs' itineraries were not invented then, but were handed down by a faithful

[1] For the nomadic origins of the Israelites, and the survival of nomadism in Old Testament literature, see R. de Vaux, *Ancient Israel: its Life and Institutions*, London 1961, 3–15.

tradition. And there were also social and juridical customs of patriarchal times which no longer existed at the time of writing, but which have been found to have parallels in the legislation or customs of peoples contemporary with the patriarchs. In other words, they were not imagined by those who came after, but drawn from an authentic tradition.

In short, the parts of Genesis concerning Abraham are popular and traditional accounts told with no attempt to give an objective picture of the smallest detail, and quite possibly mingling a certain amount of legend with authentic memory. Though very different from modern historical writing, they contain nonetheless a faithful picture of Abraham, his origins, his mission and his religious attitude.

The bones of the story, so to speak, are the calling and the promise. (Gn 12 : 1–9; 15 : 1–20.)

The calling of Abraham

The first account about Abraham describes his calling: "The Lord said to Abraham, Go from your country and your kindred and your father's house to the land that I will show you." (Gn 12 : 1.) There are various elements to note here. From the first the election of Abraham appears as a choice in which God has all the initiative: the writer does not mention any merits or virtues of Abraham, but merely tells us that the Lord spoke to him; evidently all that matters to him is that God chose the man he wanted. God's call is a demanding one: to answer it, Abraham must leave his own country, sever his family relations and go to an unknown land. The sacrifice will not be a wasted one, for Abraham's calling is directed to the fulfilment of God's plan. Yahweh calls him to become the father of a great people, and to receive a blessing that will extend to all the nations of the earth: "I will make of you a great nation, and I will bless you, and make your name great, so that you will be a blessing. I will bless those who bless you, and him who curses you I will curse: and in you all the families of the earth will be blessed." (Gn 12 : 2–3.)

"All the peoples of the earth are involved, for in his choice of one people the God of Israel had in mind the salvation of all."[1]

If the calling of Abraham was directed to the fulfilment of the divine plan, the existence of the chosen people was bound up with his response. Abraham obeyed: "So Abraham went, as the Lord had told him." (Gn 12 : 4.) It was a departure into the unknown, with no security apart from God's word; obedience to God's call was the response of faith. "By faith", we read in Hebrews (11 : 8), "Abraham obeyed when he was told to go out to a place which he was to receive as an inheritance; and he went out, not knowing where he was to go." The Old Testament opens with an act of faith, just as the New was to.

[1] L. H. Grollenberg, OP, *Atlas of the Bible*, London and Edinburgh 1957, 28.

The promise

The account of the promise (Gn 15 : 1–20) completes the account of the calling. Abraham is now in Canaan, and God's assurances have not yet been implemented. Yahweh renews his promise, and seals it by a sacrifice of covenant.

The promise has two main elements: Abraham is to be the father of a numerous people, and God will give the land to his descendants. Though he has no child and is, humanly speaking, incapable of having one because of his age,[1] he is to become the father of a whole nation: "Look towards heaven and number the stars, if you are able to number them.... So shall your descendants be." (Gn 15 : 5.)

In chapter 17 with its "priestly" tradition parallel to this one, Abraham's name is explained by its similarity in sound to *ab hamon*, father of a multitude: "Your name shall be Abraham, for I have made you the father of a multitude of nations."[2] To follow God's call Abraham had left his homeland; God promises to give the land of Canaan to the people that is to be born of him: "To your descendants I give this land, from the river of Egypt to the great river, the river Euphrates." (Gn 15 : 18.)

Reading the story of Abraham, we are struck by the importance the author places on the buying of the field and cave of Machrelah; he sees

[1] Gn 15 : 2: "I continue childless..."; Gn 17 : 1: "When Abram was ninety-nine years old the Lord appeared to Abram...."
[2] v. 5, and see R. de Vaux's note, *La Genèse*, 87.

in it the beginnings of the fulfilment of the promise, for it is the first property-right he acquires. (Gn 23.)

To God's promise, which could not be fulfilled at all, humanly speaking, Abraham once again responds by faith: "And he believed the Lord; and he reckoned it to him as righteousness." (Gn 15 : 6.)

The scene concludes with a covenant: God addresses Abraham in terms he can understand, and seals his promise by an ancient rite of covenant. Having made an engagement, the contracting parties used to immolate animals, divide them down the middle, and place each half opposite the other; then they passed between the bleeding halves, calling down on themselves a similar fate should they violate the promises they had made. Yet the description respects the transcendence of God: God manifests himself through the symbol of fire, and Abraham sees him only in a dream: " When the sun had gone down and it was dark, behold, a smoking fire pot and a flaming torch passed between these pieces." (Gn 15 : 17.)

Only God passed between the victims, for only he was engaging himself, making Abraham a promise without any being made to him in return.

Attitudes of God and man

Making Abraham father of the chosen people was, after the fall, the first stage in the accomplishment of salvation. It is also a revelation of the way in which God acts to save man, and the response he wants from him. From Abraham onwards, the history of the bible is a lesson, through events, of the attitudes of God and of man.

God does not act according to the norms of any merely human wisdom. He chooses whom he will, and his is the initiative: the election of Abraham, the choosing of Isaac and not Ishmael (Gn 17), of Jacob rather than Esau. (Gn 25 : 23.) The way in which he leads his promises to fulfilment is disconcerting to human wisdom, and forces man to trust in God: Abraham left for the unknown to follow the call he heard; God promised him numerous descendants though he had no children and was too old to have any—he had a son by his slave Hagar, but he was not the child of the promise (Gn 17 : 15–22); God gave him a son by Sarah his wife, who was barren: Isaac, upon whom the promise rested (Gn 17 : 21); Isaac grew up, and then God demanded that Abraham should sacrifice this son who was his only hope of seeing the promise fulfilled.[1]

However disconcerting the road along which God led Abraham, however much of a dead-end it appeared, Abraham retained the attitude he had adopted when he first heard God's call—an

[1] Gn 22. This account tells us two important things: God wanted the Israelites to understand that he did not want the sacrifices of children so common among the Canaanites, and that what he wanted above all was obedience in faith, of which Abraham was an example; see J. Chaîne, *Le livre de la Genèse*, 270–75.

attitude of total and unconditional faith, and of heroic obedience to whatever God asked of him. This is the response God expects of all whom he calls to collaborate in his plan.

Abraham, God's friend

Because a vocation is always a sign of God's love, and because he believed in God's promise, Abraham was God's friend. Genesis expresses this very charmingly in the account of the apparition of Mamre: three mysterious visitors come to see Abraham, and eat in his tent, and one of them is Yahweh. (Gn 18 : 1–15.) Later, in a daring image, the author shows Yahweh wondering whether to punish the sinful city of Sodom without telling Abraham: "Shall I hide from Abraham what I am about to do, seeing that Abraham shall become a great and mighty nation, and in him all the families of the earth shall be blessed?" (Gn 18: 17–18.)

St James takes from the deutero-Isaiah and from Daniel the title that expresses Abraham's intimacy with God: "Abraham believed God, and it was reckoned to him as righteousness, and he was called the friend of God." (2 : 23; Is 41 : 8; Dn 3 : 25.)

Even today, a few miles from Hebron, at Mamre, where Abraham set up his tents, the Arabs call the hill Ramet El-Khalil, "The friend's height"; for Jews, Christians and Moslems alike, Abraham is God's friend.

Abraham and ourselves

Such is Abraham, the founder of the people of God. He it was whom Yahweh chose to become father of the nation in which his Son was to become man; he it was to whom the Lord promised a blessing that should extend to all nations—a promise fulfilled in Jesus Christ, and given to all who believe in him; he remains the ancestor whose faith and obedience are a kind of living law, not only to the Old-Testament Israelites, but also for the Christians who form the new Israel.

Once Abraham's place in the divine plan has been grasped, we come to love certain phrases of the liturgy which had formerly seemed mere relics of the past; we realise why, in adult baptisms and during the nuptial mass, the priest invokes the God of Abraham, Isaac and Jacob; we are no longer surprised to find him, during mass, asking God to accept his sacrifice as he accepted Abraham's; and in the mass for the dead, we can say with a more intelligent faith: "Lord, make them pass from death to the life that long ago you promised to Abraham and his seed."[1]

It is not only liturgically that knowing Abraham makes a difference to us. The Christian who is aware that spiritually he belongs to Abraham's posterity, and that he has his own special place in the plan of salvation which God set in motion by calling Abraham, has a sense

[1] Offertory of the mass for the dead.

of solidarity with him, a sense of following him along the road of faith, obedience, and dependence on God alone.

Reading

Gn 12–24—especially 12:1–9; 15; 17; 18; 22; Eccl 44:19–23; Jn 8:52–8; Gal 3:6–9; Rom 4; Heb 11:8–19

4

Places and dates in Bible history

God's intervention to fulfil his plan of salvation is inscribed, in space and in time, in the very heart of the history of the world: it is a fact which bible readers must not fail to take into account if they want to realise the full dimensions of God's message and all its human echoes.

Bible lands

When we talk of the bible lands, we normally mean the area where the major events of the history of Israel, the life and ministry of Christ, and the earliest activity of the church all took place. Though the boundaries of the area have varied at different times, we can take as a general framework the following: to the north the southern extremities of the Lebanon and Anti-Lebanon; to the west the Mediterranean; to the south the northern end of the Sinai peninsula; to the east the plateau of the Hamad, or Syrian steppes.[1] The altitudes vary enormously: the

[1] For more detail, consult L. H. Grollenberg, *Atlas of the Bible*, London and Edinburgh 1957; or H. G. May, R. W. Hamilton, and G. N. S. Hunt, *Oxford Bible Atlas*, Oxford 1962.

traveller approaching from the west crosses a fairly wide coastal plain, then ascends the chain of mountains that runs down the country from north to south and forms a kind of spine (hills of Galilee, hills of Samaria, hills of Judaea). This chain, along which are to be found the ancient sanctuaries of Shiloh, Bethel, Gibeon, and Jerusalem, the capital, is high, especially in Judaea: at the Mount of Olives the altitude is 2435 feet, at Hebron 3320. He then descends sharply to the Jordan, which flows along the bottom of a wide rift valley running from north to south, and crosses Lake Huleh (six feet above sea-level, and the Lake of Tiberias (700 feet below sea-level) and flows into the Dead Sea (1290 feet below sea-level). From the Jordan valley, the level quickly rises to the plateau of Transjordan (the mountains of Gilead, Mount Nebo (2739 feet), the mountains of Moab). One gets a good total idea of the shape of the country if one adds to this east–west picture the realisation that, at the level of Haifa, the coastal plain and the mountainous spine are cut from north-west to south-east by Mount Carmel and the plain of Esdraelon.

To visit the Holy Land makes it easier to understand a great many of the details of the bible; once one has made the journey from Jerusalem to Jericho one can never forget the phrase in the parable: "A man was going down from Jerusalem to Jericho" (Lk 10 : 30); once one has walked for a few hours in the summer among the *wadis* of the desert of Juda one can

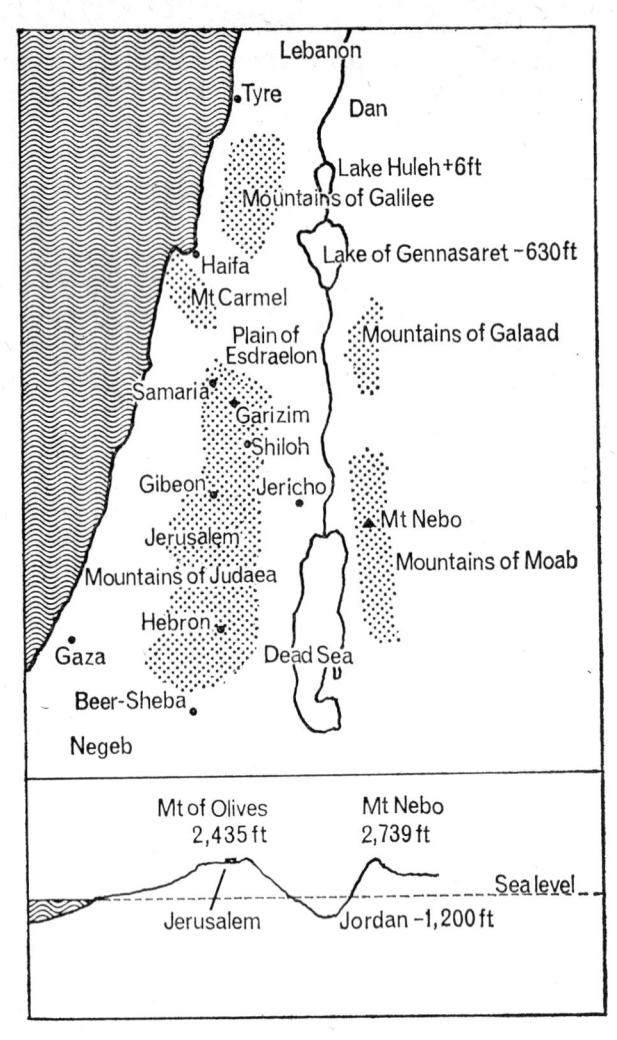

Palestine

appreciate the value of such symbols as living water and green pastures (Ps 23); once one has seen the stony earth of Palestine, and the watch-towers in the fields, this symbolism of the vine becomes real indeed: "My beloved had a vineyard on a very fertile hill. He digged it and cleared it of stones, and planted it with choice vines; he built a watch-tower in the midst of it, and hewed out a wine vat in it; and he looked for it to yield grapes, but it yielded wild grapes." (Is 5 : 1–2.)

Failing a personal knowledge of the country, which is easier now than ever before with so many pilgrimages being arranged, it is very useful to familiarise oneself with the bible landscape, as one can with the help of various illustrated books on the Holy Land.[1]

Palestine, centre of the "fertile crescent"

That land is situated in the middle of the "fertile crescent" formed by the valley and delta of the Nile, the coastal land along the Mediterranean, and the alluvial plains of the Tigris and Euphrates. The wanderings of the patriarchs, and the history of the people of God up to Christ's time, all took place in that crescent. Abraham went from Ur to Haran and then into Canaan; his descendants got as far as Egypt,

[1] See, for instance, *The Holy Land*, London 1958, or *The Voyage to the Holy Land*, London 1964.

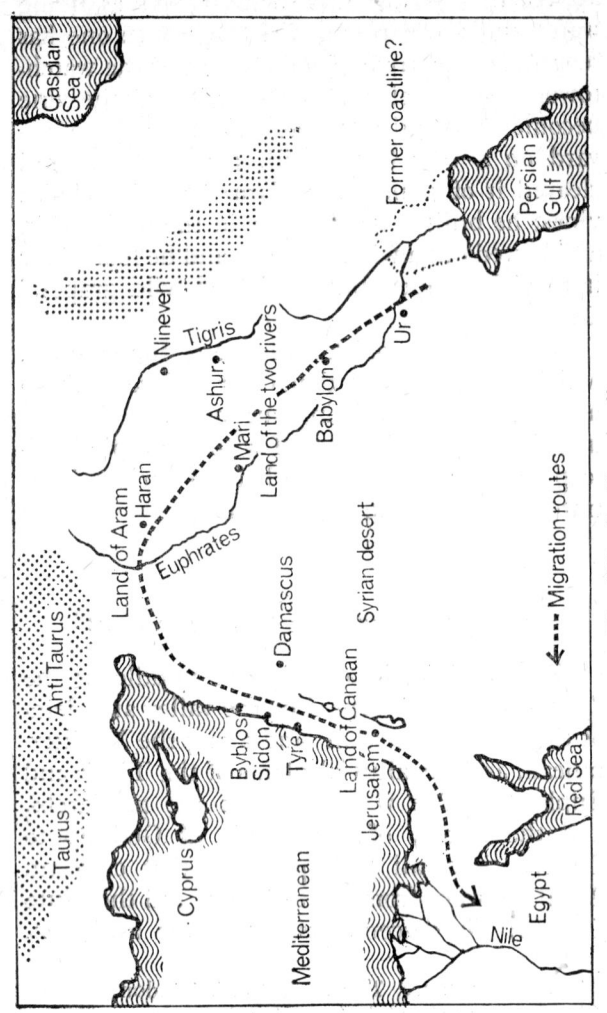

The "Fertile Crescent"

and returned to Canaan where they settled; they were taken into exile in Babylon, and then returned to Palestine.

Israel's geographical situation helps to explain its history: Palestine, as the centre of the fertile crescent, is the natural road from Egypt to Mesopotamia or the area between the Tigris and Euphrates. That is why Israel had to trace a path amid the political fluctuations of Egypt and Assyria, as well as having sometimes to fight less important neighbours like Syria, Edom and Moab.

The bible and the history of the ancient east

The bible tells the story of the chosen people for a religious purpose. Sometimes it says nothing at all about the general historical framework in which the events it records take place—thus with Abraham it gives only the essential element of his calling by God, so that, not knowing the historical and cultural context, people have sometimes been too quick to dismiss the whole story. Sometimes the bible describes the relationship of Israel with neighbouring peoples, with such episodes as the embassy of Merodachbaladan, king of Babylon, to Hezekiah, king of Judah, and the embassy of Hezekiah to Egypt. The secular history in the background helps us to understand the concrete reality and basis in history of the people of God. We know, for instance that a wave of Hyksos from Palestine settled in the Nile delta around 1720, and dominated the country until around 1570—the

Pharaohs of the fifteenth and sixteenth dynasties were Hyksos. The arrival and settling of the family of Jacob in Egypt were probably connected with the power of the Hyksos, a largely semitic people, and the promotion of Joseph to the job of an important functionary is understandable under a Semitic Pharaoh. In the twelfth and eleventh centuries peace reigned in the Near East; Egypt was worn out by its wars with the "peoples of the sea", Assyria was weakened, and after the fall of the Hittite empire no large-scale power was established in Asia Minor. The climate was favourable to the creation of an Israelite state. Furthermore, the Philistines' attempts to expand from the coastal plain towards the mountains forced the Israelites (who up till then had consisted in a kind of federation of tribes) into uniting under a king. It is interesting to know all this when embarking on the books of Samuel. Later, in 538, the edict of Cyrus authorised the Jews who were captives in Babylon, to return to their own land, and ordered that the Temple be rebuilt at the Treasury's expense, and that the sacred vessels taken from Jerusalem be restored. Such a measure might surprise the reader of the books of Esdras, but he will learn from secular history that Cyrus did the same with all the peoples subject to the Chaldeans.[1] To know the general historical context and human background of the people of God makes it possible to understand

[1] See, in connection with these three examples, Grollenberg, *Atlas of the Bible*.

the history of Israel far better; and this in turn gives us a clearer grasp of God's education of them and of the transcendence of his revelation.

The great dates in bible history

The history of the Old Testament is recorded in the historical books, but the utterances of the prophets and the doings of the sages also have their place in that history. Similarly, the epistles and Revelation complete what the gospels and Acts have to tell us of the new covenant. The various different biblical writings give complementary aspects of one and the same history. If the reader is not to be confused by passing from one book to another, he must realise which are the key-moments in the history of salvation. Here then is a table to bring to mind, in order, the major stages in God's plan and Israel's destiny. Each has its special meaning and religious part to play in the divine plan; each is part of a definite history, and has its own persons of importance—Abraham, Moses, David, and so on. The lesson to be drawn from the whole thing is that of the continuity of God's plan to save the real world by making use of human beings, and bringing the reality of salvation right into human history.[1]

[1] You will find more detailed chronological tables in B. W. Anderson, *The Living World of the Old Testament*, 30, 110, 192, 202, 240, 267, 294, 355, 451, and 521; and also in the *Bible de Jérusalem*, 1641–57 (the English translation of which is due to be published in the Autumn of 1966).

THE GREAT DATES IN BIBLE HISTORY

THE CREATION OF THE PEOPLE OF THE OLD COVENANT
The Patriarchs—The ancestors of the People of God

Dates	People	Events	Place in history of salvation	History of Near East
c. 1850	*Abraham* in Canaan—Father of chosen people		The election, the promise	
	Isaac			
	Jacob: his sons the founders of the tribes of Israel			Hammurabi: 1728–1686
c. 1700	Joseph in Egypt			c. 1720: Hyksos in Nile delta
		The Hebrews in Egypt		
		THE EXODUS		
between 1250 and 1214	*Moses*	Liberation from yoke of Egypt	Forming of people as a people	
		The covenant of Sinai	Consecration of the election: Israel, people of Yahweh	
		ENTRY INTO THE PROMISED LAND		
c. 1200	*Joshua*	Crossing the Jordan: conquest and division of country	Entry into Promised Land	twelfth and eleventh centuries: political calm (Egypt and Assyria weak)

c. 1060	The judges, liberators raised up by Yahweh	Time of transition to monarchy; tribes living in kind of federation		Philistines attempting to expand from plain to mountains
	Samuel, judge and prophet, birth of			

THEOCRATIC KINGDOM

	Saul	Theocratic monarchy (authority of prophet over king—king political and religious leader)	Monarchy in Israel	
c. 1010	*David*	Centralisation		
		David's capture of Jerusalem	Jerusalem political and religious capital	
		Promise now definitely to David's descendants	Messiah son of David	
c. 970	Solomon	Building of temple	The temple	
		Religious weakening (foreign women)		
		Social crisis (shocking inequality, taxes, forced labour) Discontent among northern tribes		
932		Death of Solomon		

49

THE GREAT DATES IN BIBLE HISTORY—continued

THE SCHISM

Dates	People	Events	Place in history of salvation	History of Near East
c. 930		Religious and political schism: sanctuary, capital, dynasty	The schism	
		Kingdom of Juda Rehoboam...	Kingdom of Israel Jeroboam...	
850	Elijah Elisha		The prophets	
c. 750	Amos, Hosea Isaiah Micah			745 Tiglath-pileser, king of Assyria campaigns against the west and in 732 against Israel Shalmaneser V Sargon II
721		Capture of Samaria and deportation of leading citizens	End of northern kingdom	
622	Josiah, Zephaniah, Jeremiah, Nahum		Discovery of "book of the Law" and religious reform	612 capture of Niniveh by Chaldeans
598 587	Zedekiah	Capture of Jerusalem and deportation	End of the Kingdom of Juda	Nebuchadnezzar

THE EXILE

Dates	People	Place in history of salvation
587–538	Ezekiel, guardian of faith and raiser of hope Deutero-Isaiah (book of consolation)	Religious renewal amid trials Examination of conscience Awareness of Israel's mission

Interiorisation of piety
The nation becomes one religious community

THE RETURN

PERSIAN DOMINATION

538–333			539 Cyprus takes Babylon: end of Chaldeans' rule. Persian empire
538	*Cyrus*	Edict of Cyrus	
520–515	Zerubbabel	Rebuilding of Temple	
458(?)	Ezra		
445	Nehemiah	Rebuilding of walls of Jerusalem	Province of Judea re-established on a theocratic basis: the Law; separation of the Pagans

GREEK DOMINATION

333–142		Judea subject to the Lagides and then the Seleucides	333 Battle of Issos—Alexander overthrows Persian Empire
167	Antiochus Epiphanes	attempts to Hellenise Jews by force; persecutions Maccabean epic	Resistance to Hellenism Struggle for religious liberty

INDEPENDENCE OF JUDAEA

142 BC–AD 63			
134	John Hyrcanus	founder of the Hasmonaean dynasty which was to be favourable to Hellenism and the Saduces Formation of the sect of the **Pharisees, opposed to any compromise with paganism**	Reawakening of Messianic and nationalistic aspirations

THE GREAT DATES IN BIBLE HISTORY—*continued*

Dates	People	Events	Place in history of salvation	History of Near East
63 BC–AD 135			ROMAN DOMINATION	
63	Pompey	captures Jerusalem	Religious nationalism	
37	Herod the Great	starts to rule	The hope of the poor purified	
			CHRIST	
7 BC	Jesus	born at Bethlehem Preaching of John the Baptist Public ministry of Jesus	Incarnation	
30 AD		Death and resurrection of Jesus	Redemption	
		THE CHURCH, PEOPLE OF THE NEW COVENANT		
30		Pentecost: missionary setting-forth of church on whom Christ sends the Holy Spirit		
70	Titus	captures Jerusalem and destroys Temple	Growth of church, the body of Christ	
		THE RETURN OF CHRIST		
			Completion of God's plan	

5

Moses and the exodus

The Hebrews in the land of Egypt

After Abraham, father of the chosen people, Isaac and Jacob became in turn the depositaries of the divine promise. Like him, these patriarchs led a semi-nomad existence in Canaan, as shepherds of small flocks moving every season, till the day when, forced by the famine, the sons of Jacob, and finally Jacob himself, came down to the land of Egypt and settled there. The arrival of Jacob's family in Egypt is linked, as we have seen, with the migrations of peoples that brought the Hyksos, foreigners of Semitic origin, there around 1720. These, having dominated the country for a long time, were to be driven off the Egyptian throne, but some Semitic elements, among them the small group of Hebrews, were to remain in the Nile delta.

The bible, which is recounting a religious history, says nothing about most of the Hebrews' stay in Egypt: for several centuries there was no startling intervention of Yahweh on behalf of Jacob's descendants, nor any new revelation to enrich their spiritual inheritance. Thus, having recalled the coming of Jacob's family into Egypt, the bible at once goes on to describe the oppression of the Hebrews: "So they made the people of Israel serve with rigour, and made their lives bitter with hard service, in mortar and brick, and in all kinds of work in the field; in all their work they made them serve with rigour." (Ex 1 : 13–14.)

The Hebrews, now quite numerous, were oppressed under Seti I (1310–1290) and Rameses II (1290–1224), and forced to do hard labour, of which we can get some idea from paintings such as the frescoes of Rekhmire's tomb (fifteenth century) which show slaves making bricks.[1] The time came when God, faithful to his promises, was to deliver the descendants of Abraham, and make a covenant with them, thus realising an important stage in the execution of his plan of salvation.

Moses

This whole period is dominated by Moses, a "key-personage"[2] of the old covenant. From the point of view of human formation, his careful upbringing, his familiarity with the Egyptian liturgy and temples, the contacts with his father-in-law Jethro, priest of a Midianite sanctuary, were all a providential preparation for his role as liberator, legislator and religious leader of Israel.

[1] There is a good reproduction in Grollenberg, *Atlas of the Bible*, 46.
[2] A. Gelin, "Moïse dans l'Ancien Testament", in *Moïse, l'homme de l'Alliance*, Tournai 1955, 29.

His calling by God is described in the bible in the episode of the burning bush. (Ex 3 : 1-4, 17.) God called Moses to a task that was to absorb his whole life, and call for a total and unconditional faith. He revealed himself to Moses as Yahweh, the God of his fathers: "Say this to the people of Israel: the Lord, the God of your fathers, the God of Abraham, the God of Isaac and the God of Jacob, has sent me to you: this is my name forever, and thus I am to be remembered throughout all generations." (Ex 3 : 15.)

However one interprets the name Yahweh,[1] and whether it was used prior to Moses or not, this name and its context in revelation express the unique greatness of God and his personal intervention on behalf of Israel.

Yahweh calls Moses to set the people free from the Egyptians, and get them to go to the promised land: "Come, I will send you to Pharaoh that you may bring forth my people, the sons of Israel, out of Egypt." (Ex 3 : 10.) In fulfilling this mission Moses would not have only himself to depend on: Yahweh was to be with him as he was with Abraham, Isaac and Jacob: "But Moses said to God, Who am I that I should go to Pharaoh and bring the sons of Israel out of Egypt? He said, But I will be with you...." (Ex 3 : 11-12.)

Trusting in Yahweh's word, Moses left the land of Midian, where he had taken refuge, and

[1] He who is, he who makes to be, he who I am (in other words, man need not know my name).

set off for Egypt once more. (Ex 4 : 18ff.) His career as God's envoy, and indeed the whole Book of Exodus, are marked by two complementary events: the departure from Egypt, and the covenant of Sinai. But before reading the accounts of either, we must briefly consider their historical value.

The exodus and history

The accounts of the departure from Egypt are all linked up with the intervention of God to set Israel free. Before we consider even the principles by which to judge their historical value, it is important to note that God's intervention is not always manifested by prodigies, but can show itself simply through a chain of circumstances so providential that the finger of God is clearly at work in them. And that, further, it sometimes seems as though the bible makes no mention of the intermediaries God uses to carry out his plan so as to make the fact of his intervention appear more clearly: when the Angel of the Lord struck the army of Sennacherib, he probably did so not directly, but by means of a plague which suddenly decimated the Assyrians and saved Jerusalem. (2 Kgs 19 : 35–6.) We find the same method of presenting God's action more than once in Exodus: the local nature of some of the plagues (frogs, gnats, hail, locusts, darkness) indicates that they were the usual local calamities but far more violent than was normal, and shows that Yahweh "made the maximum use of secondary causes".[1] This gives us valuable guidance towards understanding the nature of Yahweh's intervention in many other cases.

The accounts of the exodus, like those of Abraham, were handed down by word of mouth, and only written later, so that what is true of the one is true also of the other. One must not expect them to have the exactitude of a legal statement, but neither must one deny that they are substantially faithful to the events they record.

The book of Exodus contains memories of the great events that marked the beginnings of the history of Israel; the way in which those memories were transmitted, their importance in the life of the people, the echoes they awaken in the soul and the liturgy of Israel, and the desire to make God's action clearly seen, all contribute to give the accounts the tone of a religious epic or *chanson de geste*, impassioned and highly coloured (notice the planned way the plagues are presented, the constant direct interventions by Yahweh, the miraculous details throughout the story, the poetic nature of so much of it). The literary form of these accounts thus allows us great latitude in their historical interpretation.

But, fundamentally, these accounts contain the essentials of the exodus, and without that

[1] H. Lusseau, "Moïse et l'histoire", in the *Bulletin des facultés catholiques de l'ouest*, April 1954, 40.

the history of Israel would be simply incomprehensible.[1]

Beneath all the multiplicity of direct interventions from God, beneath the mass of descriptive detail, beneath the obvious exaggeration of situations and scenes, there are incontestable facts. They are there in spite of all the highly-coloured embroidery that surrounds them. Brought together, they add up to an event of tremendous importance. A people subject for long years to degrading slavery suddenly shook off their shackles which had prevented any hope of their ever being set free. A race that had grown weak through alliances with foreigners, and thinned out by secular promiscuity with very dubious elements, regained the idea of ethnic purity that possessed its great ancestors. A community who had let themselves waver from their early monotheism and worship in Egyptian shrines now bound themselves to the one true God

[1] "If one denies the historical reality of these data (the departure from Egypt, the religious experience of Sinai, the establishment of the Law and its worship), and of the person of Moses (the liberator, guide and lawgiver chosen by God), then one makes the rest of the history of Israel inexplicable, with their fidelity to Yahwism and their clinging to the law of Moses" (B. Couroyer, OP, *L'Exode*, Paris 1952, 10). A similar reflection can be found in H. Cazelles, "Moïse", DBS, 5, col. 1318. This article shows the truth and wisdom of A. Gelin's remark: "A little historical knowledge leads away from Moses, but a lot leads back to him" ("Moïse dans l'Ancien Testament", 30).

in a collective act of religion, and received a civil and religious legislation completely dedicated to the service of Yahweh. This people managed to find their way, in spite of obstacles that were far from slight, to the borders of Canaan, and joyfully to enter it. And all this took place under the guidance of one man who presented himself as Yahweh's lieutenant, and victoriously assumed the heaviest responsibilities. Surely this event, in itself, demythologised and stripped of all epic exaggeration (which is in any case understandable in its context), bears the stamp of God's miraculous intervention? Here we have the great miracle, analogous to the miracle of the establishment of the gospel, the conversion of St Paul, the perseverance of the martyrs, the permanence of the church.[1]

Between what is, properly speaking, the miracle of the exodus, and the details which are manifestly the embroideries of the imagination, there is an area in which it is impossible to determine exactly what is historical truth and what is not. One must certainly work on the principle that the closer connection any given element has with the central miracle, the slower one should be to doubt its historicity; but allowing for this, we must "leave the texts their epic flow and tone",[2] and remember that if God had judged it good to reveal exactly which parts are

[1] Lusseau, 40.
[2] Gelin, 37.

history and which imagination, he would not have had these traditions put down in an epic framework.

The departure from Egypt

The exodus from Egypt is one of the fundamentals of Israel's faith, along with the creation and the election of Abraham. It is preceded by a striking account of Moses' interviews with Pharaoh, and the plagues of Egypt, from which we can deduce the major fact that Yahweh, who called Moses, was more powerful than Pharaoh, and intervened effectively to force him to let the children of Israel go. (Ex 7 : 8–11, 10.)

The departure from Egypt was marked by the celebration of the first Israelite Passover. This word, of uncertain origin,[1] is related in popular etymology to the passing over of Yahweh[2] when he struck down the Egyptians and spared the Hebrews. The Pasch sometimes refers to the lamb immolated for the feast (Ex 7 : 21; 1 Cor 5 : 7: "Christ our paschal lamb has been sacrificed"), and sometimes the feast as a whole, with its recalling of the various elements of the exodus: the eating of the Pasch, the passing over of Yahweh and the crossing of the Red Sea.

Exodus 7, which belongs mainly to the priestly tradition, describes the celebration of the Passover with all the ritual details and prescriptions. By

[1] cf. B. Couroyer, OP, "L'origine égyptienne du mot 'Pâque'", in *RB*, 1955, 481–96.

[2] Literally "the salvation of Yahweh", Ex 7 : 13 and 23; see Couroyer, "L'origine égyptienne", 493.

Yahweh's command, the Israelites kill and eat the paschal lamb: "On the tenth day of this month they shall take every man ... a lamb for a household.... Your lamb shall be without blemish, a male a year old; you shall take it from the sheep or from the goats; and you shall keep it until the fourteenth day of this month, when the whole assembly of the congregation of Israel shall kill their lambs in the evening. Then they shall take some of the blood, and put it on the two doorposts and the lintel of the houses in which they eat them. They shall eat the flesh that night, roasted; with unleavened bread and bitter herbs they shall it eat.... In this manner you shall eat it: your loins girded, your sandals on your feet, and your staff in your hand; and you shall eat it in haste. It is the Lord's passover.... The blood shall be a sign for you, upon the houses where you are; and when I see the blood, I will pass over you, and no plague shall fall upon you to destroy you, when I smite the land of Egypt." (Ex 7 : 3–13.)

Note the details which indicate the atmosphere and haste of the departure: the Hebrews were to eat unleavened bread, and to eat the Pasch standing and dressed for their journey.

The sacrifice is followed by the passing of Yahweh, sparing Israel but smiting the Egyptians, and thereby setting his people free: "At midnight the Lord smote all the first-born in the land of Egypt.... And there was a great cry in Egypt, for there was not a house where one was not dead. And he summoned Moses and

Aaron by night, and said, 'Rise up, go forth from among my people ... and go, serve the Lord.'" (Ex 12 : 29–31.)

Whatever the event actually was, and we shall never know for certain, it would be a total failure to understand the literary form of the book to imagine the Exterminator as an angel striking each child in turn. The description of this disaster, like those that have gone before, is a way of expressing the reality of God's omnipotent intervention to help his people. God has set Israel free: "All the hosts of the Lord went out from the land of Egypt." (Ex 7 : 41.)

Deliverance was to be complete, however, only after the crossing of the Red Sea: the crossing of the "Sea of Reeds" was to place the children of Israel finally beyond Egyptian domination. After their first confusion, the Egyptians pulled themselves together, and rushed in pursuit of the Hebrews, but, just as their situation became critical, God intervened to save his people: "When Pharaoh drew near ... the people of Israel cried out to the Lord. ... Then Moses stretched out his hand over the sea and the Lord drove the sea back by a strong east wind all night, and made the sea dry land, and the waters were divided. And the people of Israel went into the midst of the sea on dry ground, the waters being a wall to them on their right hand and on their left. The Egyptians pursued and went in after them, all Pharaoh's horses, his chariots and his horsemen. And in the morning watch the Lord in the pillar of fire and of cloud looked down upon the host of the Egyptians, and discomfited the host of the Egyptians, clogging their chariot wheels so that they drove heavily.... Then the Lord said to Moses, 'Stretch out your hand over the sea, that the water may come back upon the Egyptians, upon their chariots and upon their horsemen.' So Moses stretched forth his hand over the sea, and the sea returned to its wonted flow when the morning appeared; and the Egyptians fled into it, and the Lord routed the Egyptians in the midst of the sea ... not so much as one of them remained.... Thus the Lord saved Israel that day from the hand of the Egyptians.... And Israel saw the great work which the Lord did against the Egyptians ... and they believed in the Lord and in his servant Moses." (Ex 14 : 10–31.)

Basically, the story is that of "divine assistance given to the Israelites at the critical moment when their exodus seemed bound to become a disaster".[1] It would appear that God made use of natural causes (the east wind blowing throughout the night). In any case, the text makes quite clear "the reality of divine help"[2]: "The Egyptians said, Let us flee from before Israel, for the Lord fights for them against the Egyptians." (Ex 14 : 25.)

This is the essential; it matters little, therefore, whether the story borrows an epic style, or whether some details betray a certain imagination or exaggeration proper to that style (the

[1] Couroyer, *L'Exode*, 74.
[2] Couroyer, *L'Exode*, 74.

wall of water to right and left, the "not so much as one of them remained" which reflects the usual optimism of victory communiqués, and so on). Yahweh has delivered his people. That theme must be the basis of the Hebrews' victory hymn: it is taken up in the Canticle of Moses, which is sometimes called the Jews' *Te Deum*—though obviously that canticle was actually set down in its present form very much later.[1]

The departure from Egypt is a focal moment in the history of salvation: with it we have the beginning of the history properly so called of the people of Israel. Up to then there were Hebrew tribes living among the Egyptians, but not a people as such; by delivering Abraham's descendants from Egypt, God made them into a people, under the leadership of Moses.

The God of the exodus

Through all the events of the exodus, God revealed himself as he had already done in the election of Abraham. The God of the exodus is not a simple God of nature, but a personal and effective God.[2] He is the one God who is behind the whole plan of salvation, the God who was with Abraham, Isaac and Jacob, and the God

[1] Ex 16 : 1–18. The allusion to Jerusalem and the temple in *v.* 17 makes it clear how much later.

[2] See Cazelles, "Moïse", col. 1324. A. Gelin puts it thus: "The fundamental intuition Moses had can be expressed in this way: Yahweh, who has chosen Israel, is the only God and the moral God" ("Moïse dans l'Ancien Testament", 43).

who saves us today. Writing to the Corinthians (1, 10 : 4), St Paul leads them to understand that Christ, in his pre-existence as Son of God, was working even as long ago as the exodus. He is a God who calls, to whom we respond, as Moses did, by faith and total commitment of self: Moses left the peace of the land of Midian, struggled with Pharaoh, and left for the desert with Israel. The God of the exodus is a God of deliverance; his saving of his people from Egypt prefigures the salvation that is to come. He is a God who saves men in community; the people who came out of Egypt are an image of the people who are to form the church, the community in which each person has his place and finds his fullest development. In short, the God of the exodus is a God of love who has mercy and saves.

The exodus elsewhere in the bible

The celebration of the first Pasch, the intervention of Yahweh, the crossing of the sea of Reeds, the journeying in the desert—in a word, the exodus—filled a place in the forefront of Israel's mind, and set a deep imprint on its religious soul. The psalmists and sages celebrated it lyrically (Ps 78; 105; 136; Wis 10 : 15–11 : 20); to the prophets the time in the desert is an ideal period, the time of God's betrothal with his people (Hos 2 : 17), and the return from exile is presented in the image of a second coming out of Egypt:

> "And the Lord will utterly destroy the tongue of the sea of Egypt;
> and will wave his hand over the River with his scorching wind,
> and smite it into seven channels that men may cross dryshod.
> And there will be a highway from Assyria for the remnant which is left of his people, as there was for Israel
> when they came up from the land of Egypt."
> [Is 11 : 15–16.]

But the exodus was merely the initial realisation of the plan of salvation, the prefiguring of the deliverance brought to the world by Christ. Thus the work of Christ is presented as the new exodus, from the preaching of John the Baptist onward, "The voice of one crying in the wilderness: Make straight the way of the Lord" (Jn 1 : 23). The fourth gospel shows Christ fulfilling the major figures of the exodus—the manna, the rock flowing with rivers of living water, the bronze serpent, sign of salvation, the dwelling place of God, the light shining in the darkness, the paschal lamb. (Jn 6 : 31–2; 7 : 37–9; 3 : 14ff.; 1 : 14 and 2 : 19ff.; 8 : 12; 19 : 33ff.)

Reading

Ex 1–18; Ps 78; 105; 136; Wis 10: 15 – 11: 20; 16: 1 – 19: 22—in this text, which is of rather a special literary form, the author lets himself develop freely with the object of edifying and teaching: to the story of the exodus, whose deepest meaning he seeks to catch hold of, he adds elements of legend or poetry, and he brings his own interpretations which really amount to a complete theology of history.

6

Moses and the covenant

The covenant of Sinai and the destiny of Israel

In setting the descendants of Abraham free from their slavery in Egypt, God made them into a people under the leadership of Moses; in making the covenant of Sinai with them, he made them into *his* people.[1] The whole future of Israel flowed from this event—it is indeed the history of the old covenant, or Old Testament. The covenant was the centre of gravity for all the rest, the central point to which the people must keep returning if they were to remain faithful to their calling. With the entry into the Promised Land, Joshua renewed the covenant at Shechem, to strengthen faith in Yahweh, and ward off the contagion of the Canaanite cults (Jos 24); under the kings, the prophets keep recalling the spirit and the demands of the covenant, and King

[1] This distinction has only a general value, and it would be wrong to make it clear-cut; the coming out of Egypt and the covenant both contributed to making the Jews the people of Yahweh. See Couroyer, *L'Exode*, 10.

Josiah, in a last attempt at religious renewal before the exile, reiterated it most solemnly (2 Kgs 23); the Babylonian captivity provoked a new awareness of its religious and moral values, and the people renewed the covenant when they returned to Palestine. (Neh 8–10.) The day was to come when the promised Messiah would bring about the new covenant for which the covenant of Sinai was a preparation.

The covenant at Sinai

The covenant of Sinai did not happen out of the blue. In choosing and guiding his people God took account of their mental makeup. To the Jews, the covenant was a mutual bond uniting the contracting parties by a force of a sacred pact, and bringing them rights and duties.[1] "**The idea of the covenant with God corresponds perfectly with the social and cultural situation of the oldest Hebrews, for whom the covenant between man and man or tribe and tribe held a most important place in social life.**"[2]

The covenant at Sinai: its atmosphere

The covenant, Israel's religious charter, was sealed in the magnificent setting of Sinai—for

[1] For example, the covenant between Israel and the Gibeonites (Jos 9 : 3–21). For the concept of a covenant, see J. Pedersen, quoted in P. van Imschoot, *Théologie de l'Ancien Testament*, 1, Paris-Tournai 1954, 238.

[2] van Imschoot, *Théologie de l'Ancien Testament*, 252.

the mountain where Yahweh called Moses is generally identified with Jebel Musa, the majestic peak dominating the plain of er Raha in the south of the Sinai peninsula. This natural setting, the manifestation of God, the sacrifice and the ritual meal, all contributed to give the event its religious and sacred atmosphere. Other elements in creating the atmosphere were gratuitousness and liberty. On the one hand, the covenant came about on the initiative of Yahweh, who proposed it to the people through Moses: "Thus you shall say to the house of Jacob . . . : If you will obey my voice and keep my covenant, you shall be my own possession among all peoples. . . ." (Ex 19 : 3–5.) As is clear from Deuteronomy (7 : 7ff.), it was not the merits of Israel that inspired the divine initiative, but simply the freshly given love of God who is faithful to his promises. On the other hand, God respects man's freedom in fulfilling his plan and does not force the covenant upon his people, but offers it for their free consent: "So Moses came and called the elders of the people, and set before them all these words which the Lord had commanded him. And all the people answered together and said, All that the Lord has spoken we will do." (Ex 19 : 7–8.)

The God of the covenant

Before sealing the covenant, God once more made himself known to Israel, as though he wanted the people to have a real knowledge of the God to whom they were engaging themselves: "And the Lord said to Moses, 'Go to the people and consecrate them today and tomorrow, and let them wash their garments, and be ready by the third day; for on the third day the Lord will come down upon Mount Sinai in the sight of all the people, And you shall set bounds for the people round about, saying, Take heed that you do not go up into the mountain or touch the border of it.' " (Ex 19: 10-12.) The day after the next, God manifested himself in a theophany accompanied by most impressive phenomena: "On the morning of the third day there were thunders and lightnings and a thick cloud upon the mountain, and a very loud trumpet blast [the violent noise of the wind during the storm], so that all the people who were in the camp trembled. Then Moses brought the people out of the camp to meet God; and they took their stand at the foot of the mountain. And Mount Sinai was wrapped in smoke, because the Lord descended upon it in fire; and the smoke of it went up like the smoke of a kiln, and the whole mountain quaked greatly. And as the sound of the trumpet grew louder and louder, Moses spoke and God answered him in thunder. And the Lord came down upon Mount Sinai, to the top of the mountain, and the Lord called Moses to the top of the mountain, and Moses went up...." (Ex 19 : 16-20.)

To the people he had brought "out of the land of Egypt, out of the house of bondage" (Ex 20 : 2), Yahweh was thus recalling his majesty and transcendence—the decalogue was to forbid any material representations of him who is the Only God, transcending all created things. (Ex 20 : 3–4.) He showed that he was master of creation and of the elements. And lastly, by asking that the people purify themselves and forbidding them access to the mountain, Yahweh made them understand that he was the most holy God.

The object of the covenant

The object of the covenant Yahweh made with Israel is summed up in a phrase which, though expressed in slightly different terms in Exodus (19 : 5–6), recurs frequently in the biblical books (Jer 31 : 33; Ezek 37 : 23; Rev 21 : 3): "I will be your God, and you shall be my people." (Lev 26 : 12.)

The covenant makes Yahweh the God of Israel,[1] and Israel the people of God. From God's side this is expressed by his presence, his support, the giving of a law and a land. He is to be present to his people in a special way: "Let them make me a sanctuary, that I may dwell in their midst." (Ex 25 : 8.) He promises them special help and protection: "If you hearken attentively to his voice and do all that I say, then I will be an enemy to your enemies, and an adversary to your adversaries." (23 : 22.) And he gives his people a law to govern their religious and moral life,

---

[1] In a special sense, for in the ordinary sense he is the God of all nations: "All the earth is mine", he said to Moses. (Ex 19 : 5.)

and the promise of a land that shall be theirs. (Ex 23 : 30–31.)

On their side, the people will keep the covenant by being faithful to the law given them by Yahweh. The covenant is not something ready-made, given once and for all; it is something moral and religious in nature, a reality which must be lived by constant adherence to the will of the Lord. That will is expressed in the decalogue, with its "code of the covenant"[1] applying its principles to civil and criminal matters.[2] The decalogue sets out their duties to God and neighbour: "I am the Lord your God, who brought you out of the land of Egypt. ... You shall have no other gods before me. You shall not make yourself a graven image.... You shall not take the name of the Lord your God in vain.... Remember the sabbath day to keep it holy.... Honour your father and your mother. ... You shall not kill. You shall not commit adultery. You shall not steal. You shall not bear false witness against your neighbour. You shall not covet your neighbour's house; you shall not covet your neighbour's wife, or his manservant, or his maidservant, or his ox, or his ass, or anything that is your neighbour's." (Ex 20 : 2–17.)

The law given by God to his people is the foundation of the moral monotheism characteristic of the religion of Israel—for belief in one God implies a religious and moral attitude.

---

[1] This is the term used to designate Ex 20 : 22–23 : 33.
[2] See Couroyer, *L'Exode*, 100 *n*.

The rites concluding the covenant

Unlike the covenant made with Abraham, the individual, the covenant of Sinai was made between Yahweh and the people; the whole people had the covenant set before them, knew the law, and ratified the covenant. This does not mean that Moses did not play an exceptional part in the events of Sinai, for he was the mediator of the covenant. To him Yahweh spoke and gave orders; he was the intermediary between God and the people, and carried out the rites of the covenant. In the Exodus accounts, there were two rites accompanying Moses' reading of the law and its acceptance by the people: the rite of the pouring of blood, and the sacrificial meal. The first belonged to the Elohist tradition, the second to the Yahwist; each had its own way of expressing the religious reality of the covenant —that Yahweh was the God of Israel, Israel the people of God.

A twentieth-century European is astonished by the rite of pouring blood, for with us treaties are only concluded around green baize with the placing of a few signatures at the end of a written document—a ceremonial which would certainly have seemed very meagre to the Hebrews of Moses' day. To understand the sacrifice of the covenant, we must try to see things with their eyes.

"And he rose early in the morning, and built an altar at the foot of the mountain, and twelve pillars, according to the twelve tribes of Israel.

And he sent young men of the people of Israel, who offered burnt offerings and sacrificed peace offerings of oxen to the Lord. And Moses took half of the blood and put it in basins, and half of the blood he threw against the altar. Then he took the book of the covenant and read it in the hearing of the people; and they said, 'All that the Lord has spoken we will do, and we will be obedient.' And Moses took the blood and threw it upon the people, and said, 'Behold the blood of the covenant which the Lord has made with you in accordance with all these words.'" (Ex 24 : 4–8.)

To Semites, blood is the principle of life ("the soul"), whether it be human or animal: "The blood is the life, and you shall not eat the life with the flesh." (Dt 12 : 23.) "For the life of every creature is the blood of it; therefore I have said to the people of Israel, 'You shall not eat the blood of any creature, for the life of every creature is its blood....'" (Lv 17: 14.)

Consequently, pouring the same blood on the altar that represented God, and then, after the law had been read and accepted, upon the people, signified a kind of community of life, a communion between Yahweh and Israel brought about by the covenant.

This is also the significance of the *sacred meal* eaten in Yahweh's presence: "Then Moses and Aaron, Nadab and Abihu, and seventy of the elders of Israel went up, and they saw the God of Israel.... And he did not lay his hand on the chief men of the people of Israel; they beheld

God, and ate and drank." (Ex 24 : 9–11.) The meal eaten in common is normally a sign of joy and peace among the feasters, and the fact of taking the same food creates among them a certain unity of life, and strengthens that joy and peace. That is why banquets were to have so major a place in the parables of the kingdom, and why Christ was to institute the eucharist in the form of a meal. The sacred banquet on top of Sinai in the presence of the Lord was the expression of the peace and living unity that the covenant effected between Yahweh and Israel.

The covenant of Sinai, prelude to the new covenant

From then on, the covenant was to be the framework of the religious education of God's people: dominated by the personality of the prophets and wise men and the poor of Yahweh, it made possible the formation of that "qualitative Israel", to borrow a phrase from Gelin,[1] whose summit was Mary, which preceded the coming of Christ, the mediator of the new covenant. In God's plan in fact, the covenant, like the whole history of God's people, was directed from the very first towards the fulfilment of the promises; it was a preparation and prefiguring of the final and universal covenant. Jesus, the new Moses, leader of the new Israel, was to seal in his own blood the new covenant—

[1] A. Gelin, *Les pauvres de Yahvé*, Paris 1953, 21.

this time for the salvation of the whole world: "This is my blood of the covenant, which is poured out for many for the forgiveness of sins." (Mt 26 : 28.)

Emmanuel, God with us, he was to be God's dwelling among men (Jn 1 : 14; 2 : 19–21), and was to give the commandment that fulfilled the law perfectly. (Jn 13 : 34.) Thus the covenant now being established was to receive its fulfilment in the heavenly Jerusalem described at the end of Revelation.

The covenant of Sinai and the Christian people

Though he has a new covenant, the Christian will still find teaching that concerns him in the covenant of Sinai. For Christ came in fact to fulfil what that covenant was preparing and heralding. Consequently, everything positive in it is to be found in a completed state in the New Testament, and the disciple of Christ has much to learn from it. Furthermore, the God of Moses is the same who has sent his son into the world to bring about the new covenant; thus the way in which he revealed himself on Sinai is of direct interest to us. He is the *one God*, who will not have his love shared with idols—whether those of today or of the past. He is the God who is *faithful to his covenant*, who does not deceive, and upon whom we can rely. He is also a *God of love*: the call he makes to his people comes from his goodness alone, its purpose being to raise them spiritually so that they may live in communion with him—and here what is true of Israel is even truer of those who possess the reality of life in Christ. The religion of the covenant, brought to its perfection by Christ, is itself an education for Christians. It is a living religion, one translated into the daily round of living; the care the law commands for the poor, for strangers, widows and orphans, are stepping stones to the great law of charity. (Ex 22 : 20–26.) And it is a personal religion, but not an individualist one, for it is lived within God's people. From the first it has been clear that the religion of the man committed to God's plan cannot be a religion set apart from life, any more than it can be an individual affair unrelated to membership in the people of God.

Reading

Ex 19–24; 32–34; 40; Jer 31:31–4; Mt 26; 26–9; Heb 8:6–10, 18

7

Prophecy and the prophets

Religious and political framework

The covenant of Sinai turned Abraham's descendants into the people of Yahweh. It was the religious charter of the people chosen to be the depository of the word of God, the instrument for fulfilling the plan of salvation in the people of the incarnation. The incarnation was to take place at the end of a moral and religious education, lasting some centuries, which was based on faithfulness to the covenant, faith in the one true God, transcendent and personal, who had called Israel, and obedience to the law he had given his people.

True to his word, God gave Israel the land he had promised them; led by Joshua, the Israelites entered Canaan around 1200 BC, and their occupation of the Holy Land which began by being partial, eventually became total. The first political set-up in Israel was one of a kind of federation of tribes, living side by side, and from time to time uniting to repel the aggression of their neighbours. In the eleventh century

BC, to help them against the Philistines and thanks to the temporary weakness of Egypt and Assyria, the tribes joined together and took Saul for their king. Their unity was strengthened under his successor, David (around 1010), who made Jerusalem, the holy city, the political and religious capital of the kingdom. Through the intermediary of the prophet Nathan (2 Sam 7), God's promises were directed more precisely upon the descendants of David; Nathan's prophecy marks the beginning of royal messianism, with him whom God was to send as a son of David especially anointed by the Lord (the word "Christ" is the Greek equivalent of the Hebrew "Messiah", which means "the anointed one". It was applied to Jesus in a completely new sense). Solomon, David's son, built the temple, Yahweh's dwelling place. After his death in 932, political unity was destroyed with the schism of Jeroboam, and two kingdoms, the northern being Israel (ending in 721), and the southern Judah, (ending in 587), came into being, developing side by side and both declaring their faith in Yahweh.

This was the religious and political framework in which the people of God lived the covenant, and in which the work of the first prophets was done.

Prophecy as a major element in Israel's religious life

At the beginning of the epistle to the Hebrews, the author declares that God has now spoken to us through his Son, having "in many and various ways spoken of old to our fathers by the prophets." (1 : 1.)

Indeed the whole Old Testament bears witness to the major importance of prophecy in the religious history of Israel: one section of the bible consists solely of the writing of the prophets, and there are also historical books that recount the activities of various prophets; and in the Pentateuch, Numbers proclaims Moses, to whom God speaks "mouth to mouth", or as we should say, face to face, as being greater than the prophets to whom God only revealed himself in visions or dreams (Nm 12 : 6–8), and Deuteronomy recognises in him the greatest of the prophets: "There has not arisen a prophet since in Israel like Moses, whom the Lord knew face to face." (Dt 34: 10.)

God spoke to his people through those he sent, and thus when prophecy stopped, it seemed to them that God was punishing them by silence: "Behold, the days are coming, says the Lord God, when I will send a famine on the land; not a famine of bread, nor a thirst for water, but of hearing the words of the Lord. They shall wander from sea to sea, and from north to east; they shall run to and fro, to seek the word of the Lord, but they shall not find it." (Am 8 : 11–12; see too Ezek 7 : 26.)

The return of prophecy, on the other hand, meant a sign of God's favour, and as the question of those sent by the Jews to John the Baptist shows (Jn 1 : 21), Israel expected the prophecy of Malachi to be fulfilled by the coming of a new Elijah just before the Messiah: "Behold, I send my messenger to prepare the way before me, and the Lord whom you seek will suddenly come to his temple; the messenger of the covenant in whom you delight, behold he is coming.... Behold I will send you Elijah the prophet before a great and terrible day of the Lord comes. And he will turn the hearts of the fathers to their children, and the hearts of children to their fathers, lest I come and smite the land with a curse." (Mal 3 : 1; 4 : 5–6.)

The prophets mentioned in the bible

Among the many prophets the bible speaks of, the "sons of the prophets" deserve special attention. They are prophets in the wider sense of the word who, though they received no direct personal call, chose their way of life for themselves, and lived near the various sanctuaries—Ramah, Bethel, Gilgal and so on. "The professional prophets—the nabis—first appear as organised bodies in the time of Samuel. They were grouped into what we might call confraternities or guilds, which traced their origins at least as far back as the period of the judges, and which assumed various forms in the course of subsequent Israelite history. In Samuel's day they were 'enthusiasts' who came together at certain times or actually lived a sort of community life. They would perform various bizarre exercises or religious dances to the music of tambours, cymbals and lutes. At times their transports of frenzy became contagious..."[1] Something of the kind seems suggested by this account of David's flight from Saul:

"Saul sent messengers to take David; and when they saw the company of the prophets prophesying, and Samuel standing as head over them, the Spirit of God came upon the messengers of Saul, and they also prophesied. When it was told Saul, he sent other messengers, and they also prophesied. And Saul sent messengers again the third time, and they also prophesied. Then he himself went to Ramah... and the Spirit of God came upon him also, and as he went he prophesied, until he came to Naioth in Ramah. And he too stripped off his clothes, and he too prophesied before Samuel and lay naked all that day and all that night. Hence it is said, Is Saul also among the prophets?" (1 Sam 19 : 20–24; see too 10 : 5–6.)

Samuel, Elijah and Elisha had connections with these groups of prophets, whom we must see in relation to their time, the world around them, and their activity as a whole. While certain "sons of the prophets" undoubtedly forgot the true meaning of the institution they belonged to, there were others who by their example made the people worship God, preserved the true religion "by means suited to the manners of the time,[2] and played a part in the battle to keep Yahwism pure in Israel. At the

[1] J. Chaîne, *God's Heralds*, New York 1955, 2.
[2] Chaîne, 3.

time of Ahab, the struggle against the worship of Baal resulted in a persecution, and a great many were massacred as prophets of Yahweh at Jezebel's command. (1 Kgs 19 : 1ff.)

We also find in the bible a certain number of *false prophets*. These were either men who prophesied in the name of Yahweh without having any mission to do so, or men who falsified God's message: "And the Lord said to me: 'The prophets are prophesying lies in my name; I did not send them, nor did I command them or speak to them. They are prophesying to you a lying vision, worthless divination, and the deceit of their own minds.'" (Jer 14 : 14.)

They attacked the true prophets on various occasions. Zedekiah struck Micaiah, son of Imlah (1 Kgs 22 : 24), Hananiah disputed violently with Jeremiah before the people. (Jer 28 : 1–17.) Deuteronomy suggests several signs whereby one can recognise false prophets, first and foremost the fact that their words do not come true. "And if you say in your heart, How may we know the word which the Lord has not spoken?—when a prophet speaks not in the name of the Lord, if the word does not come to pass or come true, that is a word which the Lord has not spoken; the prophet has spoken it presumptuously, you need not be afraid of him." (Dt 18 : 21–2.)

But it could happen that lying prophets deceived the people with prodigies, so that in the last resort the most worthwhile criterion is fidelity to Yahwism: "If a prophet arises among you ... and gives you a sign ... and the sign or wonder which he tells you comes to pass, and if he says, Let us go after other gods (which you have not known), and let us serve them, you shall not listen to the words of that prophet.... For the Lord your God is testing you to know whether you love the Lord your God with all your heart and with all your soul. You shall walk after the Lord your God and fear him.... But that prophet ... shall be put to death; because he has taught rebellion against the Lord your God, who brought you out of the land of Egypt." (Dt 8 : 2–6.)

The third kind of prophets shown in the bible are the prophets by vocation. As their name indicates, these are prophets personally called by God who has chosen them to fulfil a mission with the people. And generally when we speak of prophets it is they whom we mean. In the following pages it is with them that we shall be concerned.

What a prophet was

Nowadays, when we talk of prophets, we tend to think of people who foretell the future. Yet that is only one aspect of the prophetic role. A prophet is essentially one who speaks in the name of another, and the Israelite prophets were those who spoke in the name of Yahweh: "Behold, I have put my words in your mouth", said God to Jeremiah (1 : 9), and elsewhere he says more clearly: "You shall be as my mouth." (15 : 19; see too Is 30 : 2.)

The vocation is the starting point of the prophet's mission, and often gives his ministry its own special character: the sense of god-given holiness so deeply imprinted upon Isaiah's message springs from the vision in which he received the call of the thrice-holy God. (Is 6.) Yet being thus possessed by God does not stifle the prophet's own personality; it is through the soul of the prophet that God transmits his message, and that soul vibrates with hopes and memories. What the prophet has to say is coloured by the world he lives in, his culture, his temperament. When Amos, the shepherd, speaks of the messianic future, he describes it in terms of an extraordinary agricultural prosperity. (Am 9 : 11–15.)

The prophets are men of action—counsellors, preachers, champions of the cause of Yahweh. Their life is a struggle calling for much courage and not without its dangers. Micaiah, son of Imlah, was put in prison and so was Jeremiah—against whom there was a conspiracy. (1 Kgs 22 : 26–7; Jer 20 : 2–3; 37 : 15–16.) But Yahweh is their strength: "To all to whom I send you you shall go, and whatever I command you you shall speak. Be not afraid of them, for I am with you to deliver you." (Jer 1 : 7–8.) They do not always wait to be consulted, but go out to the streets or the temple or the religious assemblies, and announce the word of Yahweh.

In their prophesying, they judge events in the light of God; they attack hypocritical and formalist worship, idolatry, social injustices, moral corruption. They announce divine punishments which, in the framework of the covenant, are designed not just to punish, but to bring about the conversion of the people and restore them to God.[1] And, further, they offer a vision of healing and salvation. These three aspects met with in all the prophetical books can more than once be found together in a single oracle. Chapter 11 of Hosea is a typical example:

> When Israel was a child, I loved him,
>   and out of Egypt I called my son.
> The more I called them,
>   the more they went from me;
> They kept sacrificing to the Baals,
>   and burning incense to idols.
> Yet it was I who taught Ephraim to walk,
>   I took them up in my arms;
>   but they did not know that I healed them....
>
> They shall return to the land of Egypt,
>   and Assyria shall be their king,
>   because they have refused to return to me.
> The sword shall rage against their cities,

---

[1] Note that when events are announced, the prophet's imagination plays its part: "Inspired by God as to the fact, the seer is not always informed as to the time or the manner of it; thus we find an element of personal conjecture and wishful thinking. This explains the pictures given of the invasion of Sennacherib (Is 10 : 28ff.), of the fall of Babylon (Is 13; 47; Jer 50; 51) and of Jerusalem (Ezek 9 : 1–10; 8)." A. Robert, *Initiation biblique*, 3rd ed., Paris 1954, 293.

> consume the bars of their gates,
> and devour them in their fortresses
> My people are bent on turning away from me;
> so they are appointed to the yoke,
> and none shall remove it.
>
> How can I give you up, O Ephraim!
> How can I hand you over, O Israel!...
> My heart recoils within me,
> my compassion grows warm and tender.
> I will not execute my fierce anger,
> I will not again destroy Ephraim;
> for I am God and not man,
> the Holy One in your midst,
> and I will not come to destroy.
>
> They shall go after the Lord,
> he will roar like a lion...
> and his sons shall come trembling from the west;
> they shall come eagerly like birds from Egypt,
> and like doves from the land of Assyria;
> and I will return them to their homes, says the Lord.
>
> [Hos 11: 1–11; see 4: 4–25.]

To strike his hearers' imaginations and add emphasis to his teaching, the prophet sometimes made use of symbolic gestures which were at once prophecies in action and the first fulfilment of the events that were to come: Isaiah walked naked and barefoot to mime the forthcoming deportation of the Egyptians; Jeremiah broke a flask to announce that Yahweh was going to break his people and their city of Jerusalem; Ezekiel took two sticks in his hand with the names of Judah and Israel written on them to predict their reunion into a single nation. (Is 20 : 1–6; Jer 19 : 1ff.; Ezek 37 : 15ff.)

Not all the prophets left written works, either because they did not write themselves, or because their hearers or disciples did not trouble to collect their sayings. Those whose prophecies we have in writing we call the prophetic writers, and, according to the length of their writings, we distinguish four major prophets: Isaiah, Jeremiah, Ezekiel and Daniel; and twelve minor prophets. Since the distinction is based on length, its importance is minimal. As the prophets were men of action, their works show all the characteristics of things written for the moment, and consist mainly of exhortations and predictions, they sometimes also give historical evidence, and information about the prophet's ministry.

The unique role of the prophets in Israel

The golden age of Israelite prophecy was from the eighth to the fifth century BC. At that time, Israel was living through a double drama: the religious drama of the people's fidelity to Yahweh, and the political drama of their decadence and downfall as a people. "In the midst of this double drama, the prophets were the religious conscience, as it were, of the people of God"[1] and the heralds of revelation. Unweary-

[1] P. Grelot. *Pages bibliques*, Paris 1954, 99.

ingly, they recalled the terms of the covenant, thus acting as men of tradition, men of the past. But that tradition was not something dead; as "champions of the cause of Yahweh", the prophets stressed all the aspects of Yahweh's belief, the commandments of the covenant in regard to the dangers threatening Israel's religion at the time, and the concrete circumstances of life around them; thus they were also men of the present. And, lastly, enlightened by God, they deepened the spiritual message of the covenant, showing glimpses of the salvation to come, and foretelling the Messiah (many people have pointed out the importance of the prophets in the development of revelation and messianism); they were men of the future, forerunners of the new covenant and of Christ.[1] In all these ways the prophets contributed to the forming of Israel's soul, and its preparation for the coming of the Word into the world.

Various other nations had their diviners and seers, other religions their prophets, but nothing at all like the prophets of Israel. Without in any way minimising the religious worth of those outside Judaism, one must recognise the supernatural character of Israelite prophecy. This is clear from the fact that men such as "Amos, Hosea, Isaiah, Micah, Jeremiah and Ezekiel, foretold several years in advance events that could not humanly have been foreseen, and did

[1] See J. Dheilly, *Le peuple de l'ancienne Alliance*, Paris 1954, 255.

in fact take place.... In no other nation of antiquity do we find, as in Israel, a series of precise prophecies made well ahead of events and fully confirmed by them."[1] The supernatural is seen even more clearly through the prophets' personalities and teaching. In their constant struggles "against the innate tendency of their people to polytheism and against the influence of surrounding religions",[2] they preached and lived the most superbly moral monotheism. The purity of their monotheism and the moral character of all these men sent by God can be fully explained neither by their surroundings, nor their own non-philosophic genius. One can only see in them the mark of God's action to help his people.

Some types of prophet

Even a brief presentation of all the prophets would really require a separate chapter, yet it is essential to mention some of the major prophetic figures of the time of the kings.

In the ninth century in the kingdom of Israel: Elijah

In the reign of Ahab (874–853) and his wife Jezebel, daughter of the king of Tyre, faithfulness to the true religion was endangered by the introduction of the cult of Baal into Samaria.

[1] P. van Imschoot, *Théologie de l'ancien Testament*, 179–80.
[2] van Imschoot, 181.

At that point Elijah appeared. This prophet from the area of Gilead, whose name Eli Yahu (My God is Yahweh) sounded "a kind of rallying cry for the sacred war",[1] arose to defend the faith of Israel, and compelled the people to choose Yahweh to the exclusion of Baal. "If the Lord is God, follow him; but if Baal, then follow him." (1 Kgs 18 : 21.)

After his victory over the prophets of Baal, Elijah, pursued by Jezebel, and the only prophet of Yahweh left, went on pilgrimage to the sources of Yahwism, to Horeb, the mountain of God, thus indicating that his ministry was linked with the covenant and was part of the religion of Israel.

We do not know the circumstances of Elijah's calling, and his prophecies were not collected in writing; but by his courage in being loyal to Yahwism, and his struggles against religious contamination from abroad, Elijah deserves to be considered in the biblical tradition as the perfect exemplar prophet, the symbol of prophecy. We need only recall Malachi's words about his returning in the time of the Messiah, and his appearance at the Transfiguration—when Moses and Elijah were there to express the law and the prophets bearing witness to the Son of Man in suffering and glory.

---

[1] Jean Steinmann, "La geste d'Elie dans l'ancien Testament", in *Elie le prophète selon les Ecritures et les traditions chrétiennes*, Desclée de Brouwer, 1956, 97. Read also 1 Kgs 17 – 2 Kgs 1.

In the eighth century in the kingdom of Israel: Amos and Hosea

Around 750, in the region of Jeroboam II, Amos, a shepherd from Tekoa near Bethlehem, went into Samaria to announce the word of the Lord. A straightforward and honest peasant, he vigorously denounced injustices (the oppression of the simple people, the corruption of the judges), moral decadence, and the formalism of religious practice (Am 2:6–8; 5:12; 5:21–2; 6:4ff.); he foretold punishment to come: the day of Yahweh's visitation would be a day of darkness and not light. (Am 5:18.) But he also gave hints of a messianic perspective, and for the first time in prophetic literature, we find the theme of a "remnant" of the faithful escaping the disaster, and continuing to receive help from the Lord: "Hate evil, and love good, and establish justice in the gate; it may be that the Lord, the God of hosts, will be gracious to the remnant of Joseph." (5:15.)

Shortly after Amos, Hosea denounced the same abuses, but he laid greater stress on worship and religious life, and attacked formalism: "For I desire steadfast love and not sacrifice, the knowledge of God, rather than burnt offerings." (6:6.) He too foretold punishment for Israel: "The Lord ... will remember their iniquity, and punish their sins; they shall return to Egypt." (8:13.)

But the punishment will be the saving of the chosen people; the suffering they are to go through is a call of God's love to return to him. God's love for Israel is symbolised as the love of marriage—the second chapter is one of the loveliest pages of the bible, dedicated to the theme of God as bridegroom—and as the paternal and maternal love of Yahweh: "I led them with cords of compassion, with the bands of love, and I became to them as one who eases the yoke on their jaws, and I bent down to them and fed them" (11 : 4). Despite all his people's faithlessness, Yahweh who punishes out of mercy, will forgive Israel when they repent: "for I am God and not man". (11 : 9.)

In the eighth century in the kingdom of Judah: Isaiah, prophet of God, the holy master of history

A man of culture, from an important family of Judah, Isaiah carried out his ministry in Jerusalem, from 740 onwards. His message is strongly marked by belief in the holiness of Yahweh, "the holy one of Israel". He preached justice and devotion—for without these worship is merely an empty formalism:

> Even though you make many prayers,
>   I will not listen;
>   your hands are full of blood.
> Wash yourselves; make yourselves clean
>   remove the evil of your doings
>   from before my eyes...
>   learn to do good;

> seek justice,
>> correct oppression;
> defend the fatherless,
>> plead for the widow. [1 : 15–17; see 29 : 13]

He called for trust in God alone, and not in political alliances which endangered the true religion by making contacts with false religions: "Do not fear what [this people] fear, nor be in dread. But the Lord of hosts, him you shall regard as holy; let him be your fear, and let him be your dread." (8 : 12–13.) He spoke of the punishment, the Day of Yahweh, but foretold the faithfulness of a "remnant": "A remnant will return, a remnant of Jacob, to the mighty God." (10 : 21.) Isaiah is especially known for his messianic prophecies, notably those from the "Book of Emmanuel" (chapters 7–11): the Messiah, a descendant of David, will make justice and peace reign, and make Yahweh known:

> For to us a child is born,
>> to us a son is given;
> and the government shall be upon his shoulder,
>> and his name will be called
> "Wonderful Counsellor, Mighty God,
>> Everlasting Father, Prince of Peace".
> Of the increase of his government and of peace
>> there will be no end,
> upon the throne of David, and over his kingdom,
>> to establish it, and to uphold it,

> with justice and with righteousness
>> from this time forth and forever more.
>
>> [9 : 5–7]

With only a few exceptions, the whole of the first thirty-nine chapters of Isaiah are the work of the prophet himself; the rest of the book is made up of the sayings of disciples—some close, some more distant—included with his work because they belong to the same "school of spirituality".

Micah

Micah, a contemporary of Isaiah's, left a far smaller collection of sayings, but the book of Jeremiah gives indications of the effect his ministry produced in Jerusalem. (Jer 26 : 18–19.) From the Judaean countryside, Micah's concrete and direct language is somewhat reminiscent of Amos', and he is like him, too, in his love of simple people. The beginning of his book speaks of the fall of Samaria, and the punishment hanging over Judah, but the prophet retains some hope, and the rest of the book speaks of messianic restoration, returning yet again to the theme of the "remnant", and stressing the Davidic origin of the Messiah: "But you, O Bethlehem Ephrathah, who are little to be among the clans of Judah, from you shall come forth for me one who is to be ruler in Israel, whose origin is from of old, from ancient days." (5 : 2.)

In the seventh century in the kingdom of Judah: Jeremiah

Among the last of the pre-exilic prophets, Jeremiah appears, along with Zephaniah, Nahum and Habakkuk, as the most important. Born around 645 of a priestly family living near Jerusalem, Jeremiah was a man of sensitivity and deep piety. Called by God in 627 he was throughout his ministry a model of fidelity in spite of suffering. Though he loved his country dearly, he had constantly to announce unhappiness for it; peaceloving, he had to struggle continually with violent enemies; affectionate by nature, he had to live alone and persecuted. Despite the discouragement that constantly tempted him, and into which he sometimes fell, Jeremiah proclaimed the word of the Lord. His life was to all appearances a failure, but he was of major importance in the religious development of Israel, during and after the exile. He was not only the man who foretold the punishment of Jerusalem, but he also preached and lived a heartfelt religion and heralded the new covenant. Thus Jeremiah had great influence on the spirituality of the "poor of Yahweh", and was "the father of Judaism in its purest development". (See below, chapter 10.)

Christians and the prophets of Israel

Prophecy in the Old Testament and the New

In the Old Testament, the prophet, raised up directly by Yahweh, exhorted the people to show their fidelity to the covenant in their everyday lives; he deepened the spiritual message of the covenant, and was the organ whereby revelation progressed; finally, he inspired hope in the salvation that was to come.

Christ, the mediator of the new covenant, brought the law and the prophets to fulfilment in something better: "Think not that I have come to abolish the law and the prophets; I have come not to abolish them but to fulfil them." (Mt 5 : 17.)

Though in continuity with the prophets, whose hopes he perpetuated, Christ was not merely a prophet: he was God himself speaking to men, the Word, the incarnate Logos of God. Thus the Epistle to the Hebrews rightly distinguishes the time when God spoke through his prophets from the time when he spoke through his own Son. And so too the content of his message was infinitely superior to theirs: "No-one has ever seen God; the only Son, who is in the bosom of the Father, he has made him known." (Jn 1 : 18.)

Of the church Christ founded, we can say both that there are no prophets, and that there is a prophetic mission. Though the charism of prophecy is several times mentioned in the New Testament, we can say that there are no more prophets, for Jesus said: "All that I have heard from my Father I have made known to you." (Jn 15 : 15.) Yet the church has a prophetic mission: it is her job to make known to all nations the new covenant, and to remind them what that covenant requires from us, now. As the centuries go by, she studies the revelation she has been given, to understand it better; she lives in the hope of that covenant's perfect fulfilment when the Lord returns. In communion with the church and its leaders, the successors of the apostles, every Christian has his own place and part to play in that prophetic mission.

The Christian and the prophets

In carrying out this job, the Christian does not look upon the prophets as strangers, but feels an awareness of his solidarity with them; for they were the heroes of Yahwism whose influence in Israel was so decisive, and contributed so much to the fulfilment of the plan of salvation in which he is also engaged. He finds in them spiritual guides, and reading their prophecies helps him both to achieve a sense of God, as holy, faithful and merciful, and to discover the proper attitude of man towards him. Above all, the prophets' unswerving fidelity to Yahweh and determination to apply to the problems of their time the prescriptions of the covenant, provide wonderful lessons for us who live in the new covenant.

Reading

Am 2:6–16; 9:8–15; Ho 2:4–25; 11:1–11; Is 5:1–7; 6:1–12; 7–11; Mic 5:1–7; Jer 1; 19:1–20:6; Ezek 12:1–20

8

The exile

The exile in Babylonia

Despite the downfall of the kingdom of Samaria in 721, the repeated warnings of the prophets, and the attempts at religious reform undertaken by Josiah (622), the Jewish nation as a whole were disloyal to Yahweh, and betrayed the spiritual values they had been entrusted with: "From the day that your fathers came out of the land of Egypt to this day, I have persistently sent all my servants the prophets to them, day after day; yet they did not listen to me, or incline their ear, but stiffened their neck. They did worse than their fathers. So you shall speak all these words to them, but they will not listen to you. You shall call to them, but they will not answer you. And you shall say to them, 'This is the nation that did not obey the voice of the Lord their God, and did not accept discipline; truth has perished; it is cut off from their lips.'" (Jer 7 : 25–8.)

Rank injustice, debauchery, idolatrous worship of the Baals and Astartes, child sacrifices, forgetfulness of Yahweh (Jer 7 : 9ff., 18ff., 30ff.) —all these were so many failures to keep the covenant, and made some form of cleansing suffering necessary: "Therefore, behold the days are coming, says the Lord, when... the dead bodies of this people will be food for the birds of the air, and for the beasts of the earth; and none will frighten them away. And I will make to cease from the cities of Judah and from the streets of Jerusalem the voice of mirth and the voice of gladness, the voice of the bridegroom and the voice of the bride; for the land shall become a waste." (Jer 7 : 32–4.)

The predicted punishment came: in 598, Nebuchadnezzer took Jerusalem for the first time, and deported to Babylon the king, Jehoiakim, and the elite of the population. A few years later, the new king, Zedekiah, Jehoiakim's uncle, failed to keep his oath to the Chaldean ruler and conspired against him, and Nebuchadnezzer undertook a fresh campaign, besieging the holy city which he finally captured and sacked in 587. This victory was followed by a second lot of deportations. (2 Kgs 24 : 10–25 : 21.)

Humanly speaking, this brought the religious destiny of God's people to an end: the temple, the place of God's presence and centre of Israel's worship, was in ruins; the nation as such existed no longer; the capital had been razed by the conqueror, and the last king, Zedekiah, led captive away after having been cruelly punished for breaking his word. (2 Kgs 25 : 6–7.) The elite of the people had to live in exile in a foreign land, far from the country given by God to Abraham's descendants.

Worse still, the people in exile were a prey to various temptations. To see Babylon "whose glittering splendour", according to the archeologists, "surpassed that of all the capitals of the ancient world, including Athens and Rome"[1] was always a test of faith for the Jews. Perhaps Marduk, the greatest god of the Chaldeans, was stronger than the God of Israel, whose people had been conquered and their land laid waste? So vast was the disaster, and so long the exile, that the most faithful of the Jews were tempted to give up hope. Could Yahweh have abandoned his people? The Chaldeans' sarcasm made the temptation to lose heart greater still: "As with a deadly wound in my body, my adversaries taunt me, while they say to me continually, 'Where is your God?'" (Ps 42 : 10.)

And finally, though contact with foreigners might strengthen the missionary spirit, the opposite reaction of self-defence in face of paganism might lead to a narrowing of the religious horizon to include Israel only.

Yet "this exile which should by all the rules have been a dead end, was a marvellous renewal",[2] and represents a most important moment in the development of Israel.

Factors in the renewal

As so often happens in the religious development of individuals, the time of suffering was

[1] Grollenberg, *Atlas of the Bible*, 98.
[2] A. Gelin, *Problèmes d'ancien Testament*, Lyons 1952, 93–4.

the occasion for a spiritual renewal. Deprived of all that meant security to them, humanly speaking, their pride as a nation derided, their religious institutions humiliated, these Israelites who had been recently so careless and self-satisfied, now opened themselves to God. Exiled in a foreign land, they recollected themselves, meditated and returned to the Lord.

Sunk in misery, far from the temple and the holy city, Israel kept the word of Yahweh—the law given by God, the ancient traditions of their history, the words of the prophets and the early collections of psalms were of inestimable value to them, and were so many helps in their return to God.

Supported by the discreet but effective activity of the priests, the prophets were the inspirers of that return. They made it possible for Israel, though dispossessed, not to despair totally but to find once again its sense of vocation, and follow it; they fulfilled towards their contemporaries something of the role of the mysterious traveller towards the disciples on the road to Emmaus, explaining to them the meaning of the scriptures and the providential nature of their trials.[1]

Israel's religious guides

Three prophets influenced the exiled community: Jeremiah, Ezekiel and Deutero-Isaiah.

---

[1] Gelin, *Problèmes d'ancien Testament*, 94; see Lk 24 : 25ff.

Jeremiah

Jeremiah was never sent to Babylon, and yet he was the chief religious guide of the exiles. The letters he sent them from Jerusalem after the first deportations urged them to hear the word of Yahweh, and not to comfort themselves with any illusions of a speedy return (Jer 29); Ezekiel and Deutero-Isaiah took up and enlarged upon themes central to Jeremiah's preaching—hope, the new covenant and the religion taught within man's heart by Yahweh[1]; the exiles gathered to read and be nourished by the prophet's words, which were assimilated for the first time.

Ezekiel

Ezekiel, son of Buzi, belonged like Jeremiah to the priestly world; he was a priest in Jerusalem, which explains why the theme of the temple is so important in his work, and which, together with the vision recorded in Ezek 1 : 3–28, gave rise to the sense of the sacred and of the glory of God which is so marked in his prophecy.

Taken to Babylon in 598 with the first group of exiles, he was called by God in 593. He began by foretelling the fall of Jerusalem as a punishment for the sins of Israel (4–12), but after the city had been sacked in 587, he became the prophet of hope: "For more than twenty years, this extraordinary man was the centre of the fiery

[1] A. Gelin, *Jérémie*, Paris 1952, 180–81.

preaching which saved the conscience of Israel from a torment in which any other national conscience would have perished".[1]

He worked to reanimate the wavering faith of his compatriots: Yahweh would sanctify his name and save his people. (36 : 22ff.) In the vision of the dry bones, "this imperturbable believer", as Renan calls him, proclaimed the certainty of salvation: "Son of man, these bones are the whole house of Israel. Behold they say, 'Our bones are dried up, and our hope is lost; we are clean cut off.' Therefore prophesy, and say to them, Thus says the Lord God: Behold I will open your graves, and raise you from your graves, O my people; and I will bring you home into the land of Israel. ... And I will put my Spirit within you, and you shall live, and I will place you in your own land; then you shall know that I, the Lord, have spoken, and I have done it, says the Lord." (37 : 11-14.)

To those who were tempted to think themselves finally abandoned by Yahweh because of the sins of the nation, Ezekiel taught the doctrine of individual responsibility, explained the purpose of punishment, and affirmed the possibility of each one's finding favour again with God. As against the notion of solidarity in punishment, Ezekiel upheld the principle of individual retribution: "The word of the Lord came to me again: 'What do you mean by repeating this proverb concerning the land of Israel: The

[1] E. Renan, *History of the People of Israel*, London 1889, vol. 3.

fathers have eaten sour grapes, and the children's teeth are set on edge? As I live, says the Lord God, this proverb shall no more be used by you in Israel. Behold, all souls are mine; the soul of the father as well as the soul of the son is mine: the soul that sins shall die.'" (18: 1–4.)

Everyone is responsible for his own acts and will suffer the consequences of them; but everyone, even in a land of exile, equally has the possibility of returning to God's favour through conversion, which is the true purpose of punishment: "If a wicked man turns away from all his sins which he has committed and keeps all my statutes and does what is lawful and right, he shall surely live; he shall not die. . . . Repent and turn from all your transgressions, lest iniquity be your sin. Cast away from you all the transgressions which you have committed against me, and get yourselves a new heart and a new spirit! Why will you die, O house of Israel? For I have no pleasure in the death of any one, says the Lord God; so turn, and live." (18 : 21, 30–32.)

Ezekiel's work is important also in that it contributed effectively to regrouping the exiles around the priesthood, the law and the ideal of the temple, which he speaks of towards the end of his prophecy. That regrouping which, of itself, did not foster any missionary spirit and might, if external observance became more important than interior dispositions, produce something of a closed society, was none the less necessary to revive and maintain the religious life of Israel. At that moment, "failing any physical frontiers or definite political organisation, there came into being a legislative body of which Ezekiel was, to say the least, the guiding spirit, and which was to become a kind of charter for dispersed Judaism.... It would be no error to speak of Ezekiel as one of the founders or inspirers of the post-exilic Jewish community."[1]

Ezekiel, like Jeremiah, foretold the new covenant. Yahweh would let the house of Israel seek him once more. He himself would, through his spirit, effect the purification and renewal of hearts; this corrects the texts I have quoted in which the prophet seems to give man the initiative in his conversion: "I will sprinkle clean water upon you, and you shall be clean from all your uncleannesses, and from all your idols I will cleanse you. A new heart I will give you, and a new spirit I will put within you; and I will take out of your flesh the heart of stone and give you a heart of flesh. And I will put my spirit within you, and cause you to walk in my statutes and be careful to observe my ordinances." (36 : 25–7.)

In a prophecy recalled by Jesus in the parable of the good shepherd, Yahweh declares that he will himself be the shepherd of his people, and raise up his servant David as prince and messiah: "Thus says the Lord God: Behold I, I myself will search for my sheep, and will seek them out. ... I myself will be the shepherd of my sheep, and I will make them lie down, says the Lord

[1] P. Auvray, *Ezéchiel*, Paris 1947, 158–9.

God. . . . And I will set over them one shepherd, my servant David, and he shall feed them and be their shepherd. And I, the Lord, will be their God, and my servant David shall be prince among them." (34 : 11, 15, 23–4.)

God was to make a new covenant: "My servant David shall be king over them; and they shall all have one shepherd. They shall follow my ordinances and be careful to observe my statutes. They shall dwell in the land where your fathers dwelt, that I gave to my servant Jacob. . . . I will make a covenant of peace with them; it shall be an everlasting covenant with them. . . . My dwelling place shall be with them; and I will be their God, and they shall be my people. Then the nations will know that I the Lord sanctify Israel, when my sanctuary is in the midst of them for evermore." (37 : 24–8.)

Deutero-Isaiah

The work of religious renewal begun by Ezekiel was pursued, towards the end of the exile, by a distant disciple of Isaiah. It was the period when Cyrus' victories over the various peoples of the East had awoken a great hope in the exiled Jews. It was also the time when Deutero-Isaiah announced the end of the exile, and foretold the universal and final arrival of Yahweh: his message is to be found in the "book of the consolation of Israel". (Is 40–55.)

To those who were in anguish over the length of the trial, Deutero-Isaiah gave new hope:

> Comfort, comfort my people,
>   says your God.
> Speak tenderly to Jerusalem,
>   and cry to her
> that her warfare is ended,
>   that her iniquity is pardoned.
>   [40 : 1–2.]

Cyrus was the instrument chosen by God to fulfil his plans. (41 : 1–4; 45 : 1–6, 12–13.) As on the day when he led Israel from the land of Egypt, Yahweh would deliver his people:

> A voice cries:
>   'In the wilderness prepare the way of the Lord,
>   make straight in the desert a highway for
>   our God....'
> Thus says the Lord
>   who makes a way in the sea,
>   a path in the mighty waters,
>   who brings forth chariot and horse,
>   army and warrior;
>   they lie down, they cannot rise....
> Behold, I am doing a new thing;
>   now it springs forth, do you not perceive it?
> I will make a way in the wilderness,
>   and rivers in the desert. [40: 3; 43: 16–19.]

To this community of exiles whom unhappiness, national closeness and the struggle for their faith tended to drive in upon themselves, Deutero-Isaiah opened universalist perspectives:

> Assemble yourselves and come,
>   draw near together
>   you survivors of the nations! ...

> Was it not I, the Lord?
>   And there is no other god besides me,
> A righteous God and a Saviour;
>   there is none besides me.
> Turn to me and be saved,
>   all the ends of the earth!
> For I am God, and there is no other.
>
> [45 : 20–22.]

The book of consolation contains several prophecies known as "prophecies of the servant" (see references in chapter 10, below). They relate to a mysterious "servant of Yahweh", a suffering just man, certain of whose traits recall Jeremiah, yet whose nature and mission seem to be something quite outside the scope of any of the Old-Testament personalities. This just man does expiation for the sins of others, and intercedes for sinners; even his death results in a glorification, and great spiritual fruitfulness. This provides a highly important teaching on suffering and death as life-giving and it is a prophecy which was only to be fully realised in Christ. This, which constitutes a doctrinal high point in the Old Testament, is not recognised by all exegetes as being the work of Deutero-Isaiah; some attribute it to one of his disciples, and in that case it would have been written in the years following the return from the exile.[1]

---

[1] A. Robert, *Lectures sur les psaumes*, 46; see, too, the various opinions quoted by A. Gelin, in "Messianisme", DBS, col. 1194ff.

The exile in Israel's religious history

The importance of the exile on the religious level was tremendous; it has been said that this period is the key to all sacred history.[1]

It was, first of all, an occasion for the nation to set about a veritable examination of conscience. Thus the last writer involved in the Books of Kings, writing after the fall of Jerusalem, examines history in relation to the principles of the covenant, in order to lead Israel to admit their sins and do penance to hasten the coming of better times.[2] The Lamentations, written afterwards, reflect this same spiritual attitude: they express desolation over the ruins of Jerusalem and the temple, repentance for the sins which brought about the catastrophe of 587, and trust in Yahweh.

The exile was also a time when Israel reawoke to her calling: "Assisted by her scriptures, rearranged and completed, reread and freshly commentated, Israel became once more aware of her vocation; just as a candidate for the priesthood looks back over his life on the eve of finally committing himself, so the people of Yahweh reread their history. And surely God is at work in both experiences."[3]

The sufferings of the exile led to both a purifying and a deepening of Israel's faith. The prophets constantly stressed the need for sincerity in devotion, and for a change of heart;

[1] A. Gelin, *Rencontres bibliques*, Lille 1954, 73.
[2] Robert, *Initiation biblique*, 3rd ed., Paris 1954, 296.
[3] A. Gelin, *Problèmes d'ancien Testament*, 94.

they assured every individual that it was possible to find God, and begged him to be converted; they indicated the personal nature of responsibility and the principle of individual retribution—an incomplete examination when seen only from the temporal point of view, but better than the notion of solidarity in punishment widely held at that time. This development in their minds resulted in the people of Yahweh seeing themselves primarily as the people of those who were faithful to the covenant. But, further than this, living in a pagan land led them also to stress the universalist aspect of salvation.

Following the fall of the temple and dissolution of their national structures, the community grouped themselves once more around the scriptures and the priesthood—a change which was to mark the next period in their history very strongly: the people of God "were no longer a nation but a religious community".[1]

Finally, by coming to understand the providential nature of their trial and to develop the theme of life-giving suffering and death, they became ready for the revelation of God's wisdom (1 Cor 1 : 17ff.) and the coming of a suffering Messiah.

The exile allowed for the formation of an elite who, on their return to Palestine, inspired the whole community and ensured the continuity of Israel's vocation. Deutero-Isaiah fore-

[1] C. Charlier, *Christian Approach to the Bible*, London 1958, 181.

told that return in the terms of a new exodus, but not one that was to be a simple repetition of the first; for the people who returned from Babylon, the "remnant" of Israel were, in fact, the bearers of a more advanced revelation, a deeper faith, a more spiritual religion, than their ancestors who came out of Egypt. The exile marks a new and important stage in the realisation of the mystery of salvation.

The exile has a lesson for Christians

The biblical passage about the exile enables Christians to understand a period most important to God's plan; this in itself should make us want to read them. But their interest is more than merely that of historical documentation—albeit religious. Everything positive in the teaching of the prophets is of value to Christians, and should have an effect upon our lives (bearing in mind what was said earlier of the deepening of Israel's faith). Furthermore, the prophecies about the new covenant and the servant of Yahweh have a direct concern for us, and yield their fullest meaning to us who live in that covenant, and know the passion and resurrection of Christ. Finally, the exile is a lesson in itself, for God reveals himself in his behaviour towards his people; he does not want sinners to die, but to be converted and live, and when he sends trials and punishments they are meant for the spiritual advantage of those they come upon. The God of the exile is the same of whom St Paul writes:

"We know that in everything God works for good with those who love him" (Rom 8 : 28). The lesson of the exile is a kind of preview of the lesson of the cross, the mystery of suffering that leads to life: "Was it not necessary that the Christ should suffer these things and enter into his glory?" (Lk 24 : 26.)

Reading

Jer 7 : 1 – 8 : 3; 19 : 1–32; 2 Kgs 24 : 10 – 25 : 30; Ezek 1 : 1 – 3 : 21; 6; 18; 34; 36; 37; 39 : 21–9; 47 : 1–12; Isa 40–55; Ps 42; 137

9

The sages of Israel

Among the men who have influenced the religious thought of Israel after the exile, the sages hold an important place. To understand this, one must see the sages of Israel in relation to the sages of the ancient East, and to the total history of God's people; then, having traced the portrait of the Israelite sage, one can go on to study the wisdom writings and find out what doctrine they added to the development of revelation.

The sages of the ancient east

Many nations had their sages, and wisdom literature is not the monopoly of the people of God; the bible itself speaks of the wisdom of Egypt, Babylon and the "people of the East", and "the Greeks themselves felt unconcealed admiration for that ancient wisdom, from which they were well aware that they had borrowed the basic elements of their own civilisation".[1]

In ancient Egypt, wisdom literature was particularly esteemed, and formed an uninterrupted

[1] H. Renard, in *La sainte Bible*, vol. 6, *Les livres sapientiaux*, Paris 1946, 16.

tradition from the ancient empire (twenty-eighth century BC) up till Greco-Roman times. It took the form of maxims or instructions—such, for instance, as these extracts from the wisdom of Amenemope (tenth or ninth century):

> Take care not to despoil a poor man,
>   or show strength against the weak.
> Make not an irascible man your friend
>   nor come near him to talk with him.
> A scribe skilled in his art
>   is worthy to be at court.
> Do not travail to gain more,
>   when you already have all that you need.[1]

It was a scholarly form of writing destined mainly for the scribes; its intention was "to form subjects capable of conducting themselves well in life, in other words of thinking rightly and acting honourably at court and in society",[2] The books of wisdom were treatises of good breeding, combining moralising and experience, psychology and good manners, the art of living well and the customs of the time. They were dominated by "a spirit that was simply the common opinion of right-thinking people, one of the important elements in the old Egyptian civilisation".[3] This wisdom was practical in its

[1] For complete English translation see *The Teaching of Åmen-em-āpt, Son of Kanekht*, London 1924.
[2] E. Drioton, in *Histoire des religions*, vol. 3, Paris 1955, 26.
[3] Drioton, *Histoire des religions*.

object, but "reflection on the world and human behaviour held an indispensable place in it".[1] Furthermore, though the wisdom writings did not set out to deal specifically with the religious problem, religious ideas were not absent from them,[2] and God was often mentioned:

> If you plough a field to advantage, and God gives you abundance,
> > do not eat your fill from what is your neighbour's.
> It is God who gives the improvement:
> > those who try to get the better of others succeed in nothing.[3]

In Babylonia, wisdom was expressed in maxims, fables, and rather more philosophical works such as "the poem of the suffering just man" which was found in the library of Ashurbanipal: Babylonian wisdom poses above all "the problem of suffering, and the tone is in general one of profound pessimism".[4]

Given the geographical and political situation of Palestine in relation to the great empires around it, and the antiquity of Egyptian and Babylonian wisdom writings, it can undoubtedly be said that the biblical wisdom is of a form foreign in origin. In several cases it would be

---

[1] P. Grelot, *Introduction aux Livres Saints*, 105.

[2] Robert, *Initiation biblique*, 300.

[3] See Drioton, *Histoire des religions*, 27–8; the author makes a survey of the Egyptian wisdom texts in which the word *God* is used.

[4] Robert, *Initiation biblique*, 301.

hard not to admit the literary overlapping of that foreign wisdom with the wisdom of the bible: compare, for instance, Prv 22:17–28:11 with the wisdom of Amenemope, or the classical Egyptian theme of satirising trades with Eccl 38:24ff., or Tobit with the wisdom of Ahiqar, the Assyrian. In any case, some of the elements in non-Israelite wisdom could well be taken up usefully and integrated into the biblical wisdom books. Yet despite all that they have in common, the bible wisdom still provides something original, for it is penetrated by the light of Yahwism, and its morality is a profoundly religious one.

The sages in Israel

The first fruits of Israelite wisdom—sayings, proverbs, fables—are undoubtedly very old: the fable of Jotham recounted in Judges (9:8–15) is one of the earliest examples. But the emergence of sages as a class, and the appearance of a formed wisdom literature, date from Solomon. At his court, which was patterned on the royal courts of other countries, more and more sages were included among the counsellors and officials whose job was to draw up legal documents; they followed the example of the king whose wisdom was famous, and whose literary activity is recorded in biblical tradition: "Solomon's wisdom surpassed the wisdom of all the people of the east, and all the wisdom of Egypt... and his fame was in all the nations round about. He also uttered three thousand proverbs; and his songs were a thousand and five.... Men came from all peoples to hear the wisdom of Solomon, and from all the kings of the earth who had heard of his wisdom." (1 Kgs 4 : 29–34.)

We have no reason to doubt the tradition that Solomon was "the originator of sapiential literature in Israel"[1]; and this explains why the Book of Proverbs, some of whose maxims may well have originated with him, appears under his patronage.

It has been pointed out that the writings of Isaiah, Jeremiah and Ezekiel show "the spirit, and even the technique of the authors of Wisdom",[2] yet the great sapiential period came after the exile. That was the period that saw the appearance of the major wisdom books— Proverbs, Job, Ecclesiastes, Ecclesiasticus, Wisdom and the sapiential psalms. The Song of Songs, included among the sapiential books, is not properly speaking a work of wisdom; its message, recalling Israel, Yahweh's bride, to fidelity to the covenant, is rather in the line of prophecy.

The Israelite sage

A sage was a wise and thoughtful man who took an interest in everything to do with the upbringing and instruction of the people and of

[1] Renard, *La Sainte Bible*, 10–11.
[2] J. Dheilly, *Le peuple de l'ancienne Alliance*, 396; the author quotes Is 7 : 5; 28 : 23–9; Jer 4 : 22; Ex 18.

the young. He was primarily an educator and counsellor; his activity can best be seen in relation to the work of priest and prophet in the Book of Jeremiah: "The law shall not perish from the priest, nor counsel from the wise, nor the word from the prophet." (18 : 18.)

The sage proposes teachings rather than imposing them; his tone is serene and evinces a wish to persuade, to have his words accepted on the level of personal conviction. The sage gives his counsels to anyone who asks, or will accept them; they are often impersonal in form, sometimes interrogative or enigmatic, to awaken curiosity and stimulate thought.

The Israelite sage is marked by three complementary traits. First, he has a sense of reality: he is a man of common sense who observes and reflects, and his remarks are to the point:

A scoffer does not like to be reproved;
he will not go to the wise.

"It is bad, it is bad", says the buyer;
but when he goes away, then he boasts.

The sluggard says, "There is a lion outside!
I shall be slain in the streets."

[Prv 5 : 12; 20 : 14; 22 : 13.]

The sage constantly makes reference to his experience and the concrete realities of life.

Second, he has faith in God as wise and omnipotent; day and night he meditates on Yahweh's law, trying to discover the divine wisdom that is shown in creation and in the history of the people of God. (Wis 10–19.) Though human experience takes so large a place in the wisdom writings, these cannot be said to contain secular morality, and the impassive tone they sometimes take is no more than an attitude adopted "to conform to the laws of this literary form". "Even in the most ancient collections of Proverbs, the maxims, though apparently neutral, are profoundly religious, and at times are imperceptibly linked with the Torah."[1]

> Better is a little with the fear of the Lord
>   than great treasure and trouble with it.
>
> A man's mind plans his way,
>   but the Lord directs his steps.
>
> [Prv 15 : 16; 16 : 9.]

Third, the sage does not merely give a judgement of value on the world in the light of faith, but writes with a view to living in the world; this is true not only of the practical advice he gives, but also of the vision of the world he expresses which cannot help having repercussions on daily behaviour, and of what he sees of divine wisdom in creation, the history of Israel, and above all in the law, because wisdom for man is precisely to imitate God by being faithful to the law and its spirit.

All these traits come together in the description of the scribe given by Ben Sirach:

[1] Robert, *Initiation biblique*, 301.

He who devotes himself
　　to the study of the law of the most High.
will seek out the wisdom of all the ancients,
　　and will be concerned with prophecies;
he will preserve the discourse of notable men,
　　and penetrate the subtleties of parables
he will seek out the hidden meanings of proverbs,
　　and be at home with the obscurities of parables.
He will serve among great men,
　　and appear before rulers;
he will travel through the lands of foreign nations,
　　for he tests the good and evil among men.
He will set his heart to rise early to seek the Lord who made him,
and will make supplication before the most high.
he will open his mouth in prayer,
　　and make supplication for his sins.
If the great Lord is willing,
　　he will be filled with the spirit of understanding;
he will pour forth words of his wisdom,
　　and give thanks to the Lord in prayer.
He will direct his counsel and knowledge aright,
　　and meditate on his secrets.
He will reveal instruction in his teaching,
　　and will glory in the law of the Lord's covenant.

[Sir 39: 1–8.]

The writings of the sages

The sages' thinking centred upon man's condition and destiny. It is particularly interesting to follow, through their writings, the progress of revelation on the question of retribution. For in fact, despite the hope declared sometimes by the just, of living forever with God, and despite the old notion of "sheol"—a place where the dead led a wraithlike and inactive existence far from God—the immortality of the soul, and personal punishment in the world to come were not clearly revealed before the second century. "A powerful and continued movement drawing the Jewish soul towards belief in immortality",[1] which had begun and was growing in Israel, had not yet reached its final form.

Proverbs

The earliest collection of wisdom is the Book of Proverbs, so called because of the many maxims it contains. It represents several centuries of sapiential tradition, for it is made up of several collections put together, around 480, by an anonymous writer, who gave them, as a foreword, a fine doctrinal exposition on wisdom. (Chapters 1–9.) The basis of the book is com-

---

[1] E. Osty, *Le livre de la Sagesse*, Paris 1950, 25. Among the texts in which the just declare their hope of living forever with God, one may specially notice Ps 44 and 73. The psalmists express their certainty of being welcomed by God, but give no details on how their hope will be fulfilled. (E. Jacob, *Theology of the Old Testament*, London 1958, see 299–315.)

posed of two collections set out under the patronage of Solomon, and possibly in fact dating back to his day (10–22 : 16, and 25–29); other sections are variations, in a more directly human and expressly Yahwist framework, on wisdom from other countries. (22 : 17–23 : 11, and the wisdom of Amenemope.)[1] In the parts ascribed to Solomon, the author sets out to make known the means of achieving happiness. The horizon is still one of this world, and some of the extremely human considerations may surprise us, but "this happiness is essentially the fruit of moral rectitude, and a reward from God".[2] Fear of the Lord, in the religious sense of the phrase, is, for the writers of Proverbs, "the first and chief means of achieving happiness"[3]; thus the book puts forward the principle which links human happiness with revelation, and with the supernatural relationship between God and man.[4]

Job (about 450)

The author of Job brings up a rather more difficult aspect of the problem of retribution. Whether Job was a purely legendary character, or some eastern hero whose memory was treasured (Ezek 19 : 14), the author was obviously not intending simply to recount his

[1] Robert, *Initiation biblique*, 191–2.

[2] *La sainte Bible*, Maredsous 1950, xxx.

[3] Lods, *Histoire de la littérature hébraïque et juive*, 650.

[4] See H. Cazelles, the article, "Béatitude: l'idée de béatitude dans la Sainte Ecriture", *Catholicisme*, c. 1344.

history. To be convinced of this one has only to note in the prologue the extremely artificial manner in which the trials are presented, and the contrived nature of so much of the story. We read, for instance, of the arrival of Job's friends: "And they sat with him on the ground seven days and seven nights, and no one spoke a word to him, for they saw that his suffering was very great." (2 : 13.)

The author's purpose is to pose the problem of the just man who suffers; to do so he presents us with Job, exemplar of the suffering just man. He is an exceptionally good man, of whom Yahweh's judgement is that "there is none like him on the earth" (1 : 8), who is plunged into the deepest misery. And the conversation is developed to show the different aspects of the problem and all that is disconcerting to the human mind. Ezekiel had stressed individual retribution, and the author of Proverbs had presented happiness as the fruit of moral rectitude; where, in such a perspective, are we to situate the suffering of the virtuous?—it is, after all, a fact of daily experience.

Job's case shows that the principle of retribution in this life, with suffering as the punishment for personal sin, is not an adequate one. Job tries to understand the secret of God's behaviour to him, but after God has spoken, he realises that he must simply bow before it. Man who cannot understand all the wonders of nature can never penetrate the ways of God, but can only submit and adore God's wisdom. "The full meaning of suffering is a mystery which God keeps to himself"; at this stage of revelation, man only knows "that it has a divine meaning that reconciles infinite justice with the goodness of the Creator".[1]

Ecclesiastes (Qoheleth) (*about 250*)

Ecclesiastes marks a new advance. The author is a master of wisdom: Qoheleth (Ecclesiastes) means the man of the assembly, the doctor. He is a sage rich in experience, and his reflections are shared with the world in this collection of sayings: he has been called the La Rochefoucauld of the ancient world.

Job would not have complained if retribution in this world had seemed to him adequate, but Ecclesiastes goes much deeper. He finds no happiness in human happiness, and declares as clearly as is stated anywhere in revelation, that this world's happiness is not enough. Ecclesiastes proclaims "the bankruptcy of pleasure, of wealth, of wisdom, of every human effort"[2]: "Vanity of vanities, says the preacher, vanity of vanities! All is vanity, What does man gain by all the toil at which he toils under the sun?" (Qo 1 : 2–3.)

He does not scorn innocent pleasures, which seem to him a providential lightening of man's burden (10 : 17), but finds them inadequate to satisfy the aspirations of humanity.

[1] *La sainte Bible,* Maredsous, xxviii.
[2] Robert, *Initiation biblique,* 195.

He does not, of course, suggest any solution to the problem he raises, but his influence was tremendous: "By giving people a livelier anxiety over the problem of retribution, and by proclaiming the emptiness of the things of this world, he was preparing minds to receive God's enlightenment about the next world."[1]

Ecclesiasticus (about 190)

The interest of the Book of Ecclesiasticus is mainly missionary. The author, Jesus, son of Sirach, was a "middle-class citizen of Jerusalem"[2] who made use of his leisure to devote himself to the study of wisdom. The first part of the book (1–42 : 14) contains counsels of morality and piety on the virtues to practise and the sins to avoid; the second is a eulogy of the works of the Lord and of the great men of Israel. (42 : 15–50 : 24.) Convinced that the true wisdom was in Israel, Ben Sirach composed "a kind of manual of moral good-breeding that would make the Jewish law attractive to the Greek or Hellenistic minded Jews who were tempted to succumb to the refinements of Hellenic civilisation".[3] His book which was to be widely read among the Jews of the diaspora helped those living in pagan lands by providing a link between themselves

[1] Robert, *Initiation biblique*, 196.
[2] Dom Duesberg, "Le livre de raison d'un bourgeois de Jérusalem", *Les Scribes inspirés*, Paris 1939, vol. 2, 1, 2.
[3] *La Sainte Bible*, Maredsous, xxxiii.

and pagans of good will, and prepared the Jewish mind for Christian morality.[1]

Wisdom (between 100 and 50)

Together with the book of Daniel, and the second book of Maccabees, this book brings a solution to the problem of retribution. The author is a Jew well versed in the Greek language and customs: he wrote in Greek, probably in Alexandria. His purpose was to show his Jewish compatriots that Israelite wisdom was superior to pagan philosophy, since the former was given to Israel by the law of God, whereas the latter was merely human. At the doctrinal level, the book is dominated by the revelation of the immortality of the soul:

> The souls of the righteous are in the hand of God,
>   and no torment will ever touch them.
> In the eyes of the foolish they seemed to have died:
>   and their departure was thought to be an affliction:
> And their going from us, to be their destruction:
>   but they are at peace.
> For though in the sight of men they were punished,
>   their hope is full of immortality...
> In the time of their visitation they will shine forth,
>   and will run like sparks among the stubble.

[1] See Dheilly, *Le peuple de l'ancienne Alliance*, 413

They will govern nations, and rule over peoples,
and the Lord will reign over them for ever.
[Wis 3 : 1–8.][1]

The revelation of the immortality of the soul, and of retribution in the world to come, provides a solution to the anxieties of Job and Ecclesiastes; it answers the problem of the sufferings of the just, and the insufficiency of this world's happiness. This is thus the final development of revealed thought before Christ's coming.

The sages' role

The sages played an important role in the life of Israel between the exile and the incarnation: they were spiritual guides for the chosen people, witnesses of God, and forerunners of the gospel. Though, in the time of Christ, the mentality of the scribes seems to have hardened into a narrow legalism, it must not be forgotten that the sages were counsellors and spiritual guides who contributed to keeping Judaism faithful to the revelation it had received.[2] In a different way from the prophets, but just as real, they were also witnesses of God in Israel. They appeared as "the representatives of a religious but completely relevant humanism", and their work of observation, religious reflection and

---

[1] The most important texts on the resurrection in the Old Testament are in Dn 12, and Mc 7 : 12–14.

[2] P. Grelot, *Pages bibliques*, 326.

spiritual direction gave witness to an "effort to bring all human values alive"[1] by contact with the religion of Israel. This lesson, which the sages gave by the way they lived, is of permanent value. The effort to know the world, the constant application to life of the demands of faith, the anxiety to respond to the needs of our time in a way faithful to the gospel—these are the extension in the church, among clergy and laity, of the activity of the sages. Then, too, they were forerunners of the gospel: each in his own way prepared the ground, some by asking questions, and others by suggesting solutions; and it is extraordinary to see how God made use of their human thinking as a vehicle of revelation—a magnificent object lesson in the collaboration God wants of man in carrying out his plan.

Barely a hundred years after the Book of Wisdom, Jesus, the supreme Sage, was to say to the Pharisees: "The queen of the south . . . came from the ends of the earth to hear the wisdom of Solomon, and behold, something greater than Solomon is here" (Mt 7 : 42).

In the sermon on the mount, and throughout his preaching, Christ carried the teaching of wisdom to its highest point; in his person, and in the mystery of his cross, he revealed the divine wisdom which the sages of Israel had only glimpsed: "To those who are called, both Jews and Greeks, Christ [is] the power of God and the wisdom of God." (1 Cor 1 : 2.)

[1] A. M. Dubarle, *Les Sages d'Israël*, Paris 1946, 4.

Reading

Jg 9:1–21; Kgs 5:9–14; Prv 8:12–36; 19; Jb 1–2; 38:1 – 40:5; Eccles 1:12 – 2:26; 12:1–8; Sir 3:30 – 4:10; 24:1–34; 34:1–11; 48:1–11; Wis 2:21 – 3:12; 5:14–16; 9; Ps 119

10

The poor of Yahweh

Like the prophets and sages, the "poor of Yahweh" exercised a considerable influence upon the religious history of the chosen people. After the exile they made a profound imprint on the soul of Israel, and the sermon on the mount was to be Christ's response to their religious aspirations. To understand the part they played in Israel's story, and the spiritual lessons they taught, it is necessary to see them in the context of the religious movement they belonged to; but first, we must indicate some possible misinterpretations in this study, and give the meaning of the terms most often used in the bible vocabulary of poverty.

Pitfalls to avoid

There are several errors to be avoided in the biblical study of the idea of poverty. The first is to give "a blanket apologia for (material) poverty, which can only end in condemning both God's creation and man's handiwork"[1];

[1] L. Bouyer, "L'appel du Christ à la pauvreté", in *La pauvreté*, Paris 1952, 13.

this is Ebionism,[1] which contradicts what the bible has to say of the goodness of the creation and work of man (see chapter 2 above), and which, by turning material poverty into an absolute rather than a means of making oneself more open to God, gives a clear field to Pharisaism and other unevangelical excesses. On the other hand, one can be so tempted to spiritualise the notion of poverty as to make it totally independent of material poverty. Such a disincarnation of poverty is far from biblical, and opens the way to a lot of illusions, if not to egoism itself. When Christ declared: "It is easier for a camel to go through the eye of a needle than for a rich man to enter the kingdom of God" (Mk 10 : 25), it is a betrayal of his thought to "enlarge the hole of the needle and shrink the camel so much that there is no paradox left".[2]

Another pitfall is the anachronism of approaching the bible writings on poverty without taking into consideration the period when they were composed. Of course the basic requirements were the same then as today, but one must not forget that an explicit belief in retribution in the world to come came late in the Old Testament, that its moral teaching had not reached the perfection of the gospel, that awareness of social problems was less advanced than now, and that these works were written in a context very different from ours. We must not therefore

[1] From the Hebrew word *'ébyôn*, meaning the poor man who looks with envy upon the rich.
[2] Bouyer, *La Pauvreté*, 14.

expect to find in the literature of poverty any practical suggestions to be taken literally, but rather a spirit, a spiritual dimension, values that hold good in all circumstances—and all this we can translate for ourselves into concrete attitudes adapted to the situation we live in now.

The vocabulary of poverty

There is a fairly rich vocabulary of poverty.[1] Two terms in it deserve special attention: *'ani* and *'anaw*, which are generally translated as "poor". They come from the same root, the verb *'anah*, which expresses the idea of diminishing, humiliation, being overwhelmed.[2] The *'ani* is "he who bows his head beneath the blow of fate, the blows of misery and affliction"[3]; in a religious sense, he is the humble man, the man who accepted his lowliness in submission to God's will. The word *'anaw*, generally to be found in the plural, *'anawim*, has essentially the same meaning; it is used most frequently in the religious sense to mean those who are poor in spirit, humble, who accept their littleness in faith and fidelity to Yahweh. The religious use of these words, which was to become normal after the exile, can be found as early as the prophet Zephaniah around the year 630.

[1] For a general analysis, consult, "Le Dieu des pauvres", in the quarterly review, *Evangile*, 5, 48–51; or A. Gelin, *Les pauvres de Yahweh*, Paris 1953, 19ff.

[2] The root meaning of *'anah* is to be bowed or bent.

[3] "Le Dieu des pauvres," 50.

The spirituality of the poor in the movement of history

The spirituality of the poor was no sudden discovery; it grew gradually out of the requirements of the covenant as recalled by the prophets, from the religious experiences of Israel in times of trial, and from the development of revelation.

The God of the poor and his law

To begin with, there is the revelation of God's mercy and the law he gives his people. By setting his people free from the yoke of Egypt, Yahweh showed himself as a "God merciful and gracious" (Ex 34 : 6), and revealed his goodness to the humble and the oppressed: "I have heard the groaning of the people of Israel whom the Egyptians hold in bondage." (6 : 5.)

The Israelite then, if he is to be faithful to the covenant, must show himself, like his God, good to the weak, particularly to strangers, orphans, widows, the poor: "You shall not oppress a stranger; you know the heart of a stranger, for you were strangers in the land of Egypt." (23 : 9.)

This command from the code of the covenant is taken up again, in the same spirit, in Deuteronomy and Leviticus: "You shall not pervert the justice due to the sojourner or to the fatherless, or take a widow's garment in pledge; but you shall remember that you were a slave in Egypt and the Lord your God redeemed you from there." (Dt 24 : 17-18.) "And if your brother becomes poor, and cannot maintain himself with you, you shall maintain him; as a stranger and a sojourner he shall live with you.... You shall not lend him your money at interest, nor give him your food for profit. I am the Lord your God who brought you forth out of the land of Egypt to give you the land of Canaan and to be your God." (Lev 25 : 35-8.)

The care for the poor and weak, which characterised Israelite legislation and the preaching of the prophets, was not just a humanitarian reflex, a simple reaction of social justice and human goodness; it was the transposition onto a human level of the mercy of God himself towards the weak and the oppressed. The Israelite's attitude to his brother reflected Yahweh's attitude to Israel; it was based on the active goodness of **God**.

The prophets of the time of the kings, and wealth

Given all this, the prophets' attitude to wealth needs no explaining. At the time of the kings, they attacked two principal abuses in the use of material goods. In the first place, the oppression of the weak, the corruption of the judges and the social injustices around them led Amos and Isaiah to condemn in the strongest terms the avid pursuit of riches without regard to the rights of the poor:

> Because they sell the righteous for silver,
>   and the needy for a pair of shoes—
> they that trample the head of the poor
>   into the dust of the earth,
>   and turn aside the way of the afflicted ...
> Also I brought you up out of the land of Egypt,
>   and led you forty years in the wilderness,
>   to possess the land of the Amorite ...
> Behold, I will press you down in your place ...
>
>   [Am 2 : 6–13; cf. 5 : 11ff.]

We find similar reproaches in Isaiah:

> The Lord enters into judgment
>   with the elders and princes of his people.
> It is you who have devoured the vineyard,
>   the spoil of the poor is in your houses.
> What do you mean by crushing my people,
>   by grinding the face of the poor?
>
>   [Is 3 : 14–15.]

The second abuse attacked by the prophets is that of using goods given by God to be unfaithful towards him. Instead of thanking Yahweh for the goods they possess, the Israelites more than once yielded to the attractions of the Canaanite fertility cults—as though their wealth came from Baal, and not from Yahweh alone:

> She [Israel, bride of Yahweh] said, I will go
>   after my lovers,
>   who give me my bread and my water,
> my wool, my flax, my oil, and my drink ...

> And she did not know
>> that it was I who gave her
>> the grain, the wine and the oil,
>> and who lavished upon her silver,
>> and gold which they used for Baal.
> Therefore I will take back
> my grain in its time,
> and my wine in its season ... [Hos 2 : 5, 8–9.]

The punishment announced, which was to lead to renewal, hinted at "the idea that deprivation of goods—though they are still recognised as gifts of God—might be the necessary way to rediscover God".[1] Nonetheless, before the exile, the idea of poverty "was not canonised as though of itself it expressed a religious ideal to which all should tend by getting rid of their wealth. Like all the Israelites of their time, the prophets thought highly of wealth; it was, in their eyes, normally a reward for virtue, and consequently they saw the eschatological period as one of both moral perfection and material abundance."[2]

Zephaniah, the first prophet of poverty

Among the pre-exilic prophets, Zephaniah is in the forefront of the history of the 'anawim, for with him the idea of poverty took an explicitly religious direction. Around 630, this prophet used the vocabulary of poverty in a strictly religious sense; he called his contemporaries to spiritual poverty, and identified the

[1] Bouyer, *La Pauvreté*, 17.
[2] Robert, *Cours sur les psaumes*, 42; see Hos 2 : 21-3.

messianic people with a people of the poor. He urged his compatriots to poverty, and presented it to them as the only hope of escaping punishment:

> Seek ye the Lord
>   all ye humble (*'anawim*) of the land
>   you who do his commands:
> Seek righteousness, seek humility (*'anawah*);
>   perhaps you may be hidden
>   on the day of the wrath of the Lord.
>
> [Zeph 2 : 3.]

Furthermore, he declares that the "remnant", the people who are to receive the messianic blessing, will be a people of the poor:

> On that day...
> I will remove from your midst
>   your proudly exultant ones...
> For I will leave in the midst of you
>   a people humble (*'ani*) and lowly.
> They shall seek refuge in the name of the Lord
>   those who are left in Israel;
> They shall do no wrong, and utter no lies,
>   nor shall there be found in their mouth a deceitful tongue:
> For they shall pasture, and lie down,
>   and none shall make them afraid.
>
> [Zeph 3 : 11–13.]

In spite of the insecurity and humiliation of the kingdom of Judah at the time of Zephaniah, it is clear that the poverty spoken of by the prophet is not purely, nor principally, material; though it has social implications, it is primarily religious, for it consists in seeking God, trusting him, being faithful to the covenant, in righteousness and humility. This idea of poverty was to become general after the exile: three types of poor man—Jeremiah, the "servant of Yahweh", and Job—expressed this ideal most clearly, and contributed to the spreading in Israel of the spirituality of the *'anawim*.

Jeremiah, "father of the poor"[1]

Jeremiah, defender of the poor (see 22:13ff.) did not belong to the poorer class, but was so persecuted, so hated for his preaching, and met with so many failures, that he lived in a state of insecurity more painful than any material poverty, in addition to becoming poor in fact. In his "confessions" (11:18–12:6; 15:10–21; 17:12–18; 18:18–23:20:7–18), written after 610—i.e., after the break in the Yahwist renewal—, Jeremiah gave free utterance to his own poverty of spirit. He suffered, and lamented his sufferings bitterly:

> Cursed be the day
>   on which I was born!
> The day when my mother bore me,
>   let it not be blessed! ...

[1] The expression is Gelin's, in *Jérémie*, Paris 1952, 183.

> Why did I come forth from the womb
> > to see toil and sorrow,
> > and spend my days in shame? [20 : 14, 18.]

> O Lord, thou hast deceived me,
> > and I was deceived: ...
> > the word of the Lord has become for me
> > a reproach and derision all day long.
> > > [20 : 7-8.]

But amid all his sufferings and persecutions, he remained faithful to Yahweh, and kept a perfect trust in him:

> The Lord is with me as a dread warrior...
> O Lord of hosts, who triest the righteous,
> > who seest the heart and the mind,
> Let me see thy vengeance upon them,
> > for to thee I have committed my cause.
> > > [20 : 11-12.]

Suffering is for the prophet "the occasion for openness and poverty of soul, for a mystical dialogue expressing confidence and the joy of believing".[1] Thus Jeremiah appears as a genuine exemplar of the poor man. His religious physiognomy was to have a great influence on the community of the poor after the exile, and especially on the psalmists. The *'anawim* can be seen as a kind of "democratisation of Jeremiah's conscience".[2]

---

[1] Gelin, *Jérémie*, 184.
[2] Gelin, *Jérémie*, 183.

The Servant of Yahweh, poor man par excellence

During the exile, or shortly after the return to Israel, the Old Testament gives a new picture of the poor man—that of the Servant of Yahweh. The prophecies about him (Is 42 : 1–7; 49 : 1–6; 50 : 1–7; 52 : 13–53 : 12) outline a portrait which was fully realised only in Christ. The Servant appears as "the supreme exemplar of the man who is poor for God, and who will bring about the salvation of all nations".[1] This just and innocent "Servant of Yahweh" has "done no violence and there was no deceit in his mouth". He is bowed down by suffering and is despised: "He had no form or comeliness that we should look at him, and no beauty that we should desire him. He was despised and rejected by men; a man of sorrows and acquainted with grief; and as one from whom men hide their faces he was despised and we esteemed him not."

Yet amid all this suffering, he remains silent and humble: "He was oppressed and he was afflicted, yet he opened not his mouth; like a lamb that is led to the slaughter."

Further still, his death, accepted freely for the sins of all, will be a source of salvation for many: "He was wounded for our transgressions, he was bruised for our iniquities; upon him was the chastisement that made us whole, and with his stripes we are healed."

The sufferings of this poor man, which are to justify sinners, will be followed for him by a

[1] "Le Dieu des pauvres", 28.

mysterious glorification: "When he makes himself an offering for sin, he shall see his offspring, he shall prolong his days; the will of the Lord shall prosper in his hand; he shall see the fruit of the travail of his soul, and be satisfied; by his knowledge shall the righteous one, my servant, make many to be accounted righteous...." (All these quotations are from Is 52–53.)

The Servant of Yahweh is the highest expression of the ideal of poverty to be found in the Old Testament: Christ's disciples were not slow to recognise in the dead and risen Christ this poor man spoken of by Isaiah's far-off disciple.

Job, "literary and theological" exemplar of the poor man[1]

In the first half of the fifth century, the author of the book of Job also gives us a religious picture of the poor man in the person of his hero. As well as its contribution to the problem of the suffering of the just, this book also contains a lesson on poverty. Job is not only good to the poor (Jb 29 : 11–17), but is poor himself in every sense of the word: he has lost all his possessions, suffers in his body and in his affections; he is innocent, and after arguing with his three friends and listening to God, he gives up the thought of protesting his justice to God, and accepts in humility and silence his state of suffering, in an attitude of faith in the holiness and justice of God:

[1] Robert, *Initiation biblique*, 49.

> I know that thou canst do all things,
> and that no purpose of thine can be thwarted.
> Who is this that hides counsel without knowledge?
> Therefore I have uttered what I did not understand,
> things too wonderful for me, which I did not know....
> I had heard of thee by the hearing of the ear,
> but now my eye sees thee;
> therefore I despise myself,
> and repent in dust and ashes. [42 : 2–6.][1]

For this Job must be considered to have a place in the total biblical tradition as one of the finest expressions of the essence of the *'anawim*.

The poor of Yahweh

The first exiles to return to Jerusalem from Babylon were drawn from among the poorest to have been deported. In spite of the difficulties of all kinds which they met with, this group of faithful believers, trained in suffering and self-denial, were the nucleus of the religious restoration of Israel. Henceforward, until the time of Christ, and especially during periods of persecution, the poor of Yahweh were to be living witnesses to the religion of the covenant.

To understand them, we must refer to the great figures in whom they found their religious

[1] For a similar interpretation, see A. Lefèvre, art. "Job, Le livre de" in *DBS*, 4, col. 1096.

attitude expressed—Jeremiah, the Servant of Yahweh and Job. We must also read and meditate on what may be called the literature of the poor, the passages in the prophetic and sapiential books which express their spirit; the psalms of the *'anawim* (22, 35, 55, etc.), the thanksgiving hymn at the end of Ecclesiasticus (Sir 51 : 1–12), the third Lamentation, one of the loveliest poems there is about poverty. (Lam 3 : 1–66.) Outside the bible, such texts as the "Psalms of Solomon", or the writings of Qumran, will also help us to understand the mentality of these poor men: "In my tribulations, I have called upon the name of the Lord, I have hoped in the help of the God of Jacob, and I have been saved; for thou, O God, art the hope and refuge of the poor."[1]

With these texts, and the history of the *'anawim* to draw on, it is possible to reconstruct the major traits of the poor man of God. First and foremost is a genuine poverty, or its equivalent—such as suffering or persecution: "Though the word 'poor' has acquired a religious meaning, one must not completely forget its first meaning; it is from among the poor that God's

---

[1] Psalms of Solomon, 15 : 1–2, 5, 10 : 7, 18 : 3. Qumran writings: Rule 10, 11–17, 11, 12–15; Ps C, Ps B: "Thou hast freed this hapless soul from the ... men who sought to destroy me and spill my blood in thy service. Little did they know that my steps were ordered of thee." *The Scriptures of the Dead Sea Sect*, London 1957, 138–9; see also 86–7.

seekers are normally drawn."[1] It is also from the notion of material poverty that the notion of religious poverty was reached, and this came about by a succession of national or personal trials. There is therefore good reason to regard material poverty as an essential characteristic of the *'anawim* as a whole. Certainly the religious aspect of poverty is the more important one, and it is essential to stress the fact. In his relationships with others, the poor man, faithful to the law, is marked by his brotherly devotion to the lowly, and protectiveness towards the weak. Towards God his attitude is one of total and sincere humility, coupled with perfect faith and confidence in him who is holy, faithful, just and merciful. On various occasions, that faith is expressed in a prayer that the wicked be punished; if we are not to be shocked by this, we must remember that the requirements of morality had not yet reached the perfection of the gospels, and that these prayers are often more understandable given the authors' ideas of retribution in this world. The *'anaw* is further characterised by his hope in a salvation to come, and a Messiah promised by Yahweh. The Messiah he awaits is humble (Zech 9 : 9), the friend of the weak (Is 11 : 3–4), and will bring the good news of salvation to the poor. (Is 61 : 1–3.) Thus understood, "poverty" is not just one virtue among many, but a religious attitude of one's

[1] A. Descamps, quoted by D. J. Dupont in *Les Béatitudes: le problème littéraire, le message doctrinal*, Louvain 1954, 147.

whole being made receptive to God and calling upon him. Of this poverty of the *'anawim* it has been aptly said that material poverty is its most favourable seed-bed, that humility is its soul, and that it is a nuance of faith.[1]

Mary, high point of the hope of the poor

The gospel shows us a few *'anawim*—the old man Simeon, Anna the prophetess, John the Baptist, and above all, Mary. (Lk 1–3.) The aspirations of the poor find in her their highest point and their most authentic expression. "She takes to herself all their capacity of receiving the God who is coming; she sums up that vast expectation which is the spiritual dimension of Israel, finally about to give birth to Christ."[2] There is in her a humility, a complete readiness, an openness to God, for which all the poor of the Old Testament had been preparing, and which explain why Mary responded so freely and spontaneously from the first to God's call: "Behold I am the handmaid of the Lord; let it be to me according to your word." (Lk 1 : 38.)

In the Magnificat, her "hymn of poverty", she speaks as "the woman who has totally absorbed the spirit of the *'anawim* as to be its most responsive and perfect expression when the newness of the Incarnation burst upon her".[3]

[1] Gelin, *Les pauvres de Yahvé*, 10.
[2] Gelin, *Les Pauvres de Yahvé*, 123.
[3] Gelin, *Les Pauvres de Yahvé*, 125.

Christ, the poor man of God

From the start of his ministry, with his proclamation of the beatitudes, Jesus revealed himself as the Messiah of the poor, and sanctioned poverty as the way of approaching the kingdom of God: "Blessed are the poor in spirit, for theirs is the kingdom of heaven." (Mt 5 : 3.)[1]

Having "nowhere to lay his head" (Mt 8 : 20), Christ lived in poverty, suffering and abandonment, in the continuing acceptance of the will of his Father and the love of mankind, up to the point of the supreme sacrifice: "Though he was rich, yet for your sake he became poor, so that by his poverty you might become rich", says St Paul (2 Cor 8: 9). He is the poor man whose sacrifice obtains salvation, and whom we must follow by becoming poor if we are to enter the kingdom.

The relevance of the lesson of the poor

Making himself poor to follow Christ, the Christian must obviously take account of the perfection for which Jesus raised this spirituality of the poor. Prayers in which Yahweh is asked to punish the enemy can hardly be taken over lock, stock and barrel by anyone who has heard the new commandment. (Jn 8 : 34–5.) But all

---

[1] This "beatification" of the poor is not synonymous with a beatification of poverty: except in exceptional cases, real misery is a condition of such hopelessness that it is an obstacle to religious life, because it is an obstacle to the normal functioning of human life.

that is positive in the history and spirituality of the *'anawim* remains relevant for Christians today, and should help them in living their poverty.

Helped by the message of the *'anawim* and with the image of Christ the poor man constantly before him, the Christian's attitude to wealth will be marked by a refusal to take advantage of a neighbour's difficulties to improve his own situation, or to make use of God's gifts for ends contrary to his love. Far from considering wealth as anything but a means of service, and from making worldly success the object of his life, he knows that the normal situation in which to be receptive to God is that of poverty, and that he can only be a disciple of a God who made himself poor by bringing a certain austerity into his life: "Who ever supposed Christianity was a viable arrangement, except people who have grown accustomed to worshipping God and Mammon?"[1]

It sometimes happens that a complete renunciation of this world's goods presents itself to a Christian as the necessary condition for following Christ's call. His attitude to the poor is one of brotherhood, resulting not merely from his sense of man as a being created in God's image, but also from his faith in the God of mercy who has set Israel free and given his only Son to save the world; such an attitude has nothing of paternalism in it, for he knows that he himself is also the object of that mercy. Towards

[1] Daniélou, *The Lord of History*, 74.

God he is wholly humble, knowing that "everything is a gift",[1] and that even his free response to the Lord who saves him is a grace from God: "What have you that you did not receive? If then you received it, why do you boast as if it were not a gift?" (1 Cor 4 : 7.)

This humility is matched only by the imperturbable faith and trust the Christian places in God, in spite of the obscurities, sufferings and contradictions of life:

> The Lord is my shepherd, I shall not want...
> He leads me in paths of righteousness
>   for his name's sake.
> Even though I walk through the valley of the
>   shadow of death,
>   I fear no evil;
>   for thou art with me;
> thy rod and thy staff,
>   they comfort me.   [Ps 23 : 1–4.]

Reading

Ex 22: 20–26; Is 52: 13 – 53: 12; Dt 24: 17–22; Jb 42: 1–6; Lev 25: 35–55; Ps 22; Zeph 2: 1–3; 3: 11–20; Lam 3: 1–66; Jer 20: 7–13; Lk 1: 26–56; Mt 5: 3–12

[1] Georges Bernanos, *Diary of a Country Priest*, London 1956.

11

Christ

> When the time had fully come, God sent forth his Son, born of woman, born under the Law, to redeem those who were under the law, so that we might receive adoption as sons [Gal 4 : 4–5].

Christ in continuity with the history of salvation

One cannot read the New Testament without noting how Christ continues the unfolding of the history of salvation. Indeed he is in continuity with the history of the universe; the Word made flesh is the creator of the world: "All things were made through him and without him was not anything. ... He was in the world and the world was made through him, yet the world knew him not. (Jn 1 : 3, 10.)

He is in continuity with the history of mankind; to make this clear, Luke takes Christ's genealogy back not merely to Abraham, father of the chosen people, but to Adam, father of the human race: "Jesus ... son of David ... son of Abraham ... son of Adam. ..." (Lk 3 : 23–8.)

He is in continuity with the history of the people of God: from the first verse of the gospel,

Matthew makes this clear by the two names he uses to sum up Christ's genealogy: "The genealogy of Jesus Christ, the son of David, the son of Abraham." (Mt 1 : 1.) He is the "son of David"—the Messiah spoken of in prophecy; he is the "son of Abraham"—who fulfils the promise given to the Patriarch. That is what Mary sings at the end of the Magnificat:

> He who is mighty...
> has helped his servant Israel,
> in remembrance of his mercy,
> as he spoke to our fathers,
> to Abraham and to his posterity for ever.
> [Lk 1 : 54–5.]

Jesus himself declares that he has come not to destroy the old covenant, but to fulfil it: "Think not that I have come to abolish the law and the prophets; I have come not to abolish them, but to fulfil them." This fulfilling is important: Christ does not mean it simply in the sense of observing them, but of accomplishing them by bringing them to perfection, by fully realising them. Thus Christ's work is at once in continuity and discontinuity with the Old Testament: he fulfils the law and the prophets, but in a reality which is far beyond anything that might have been hoped for from them.

There is no hiatus in the history of salvation, but the carrying on of the same plan, which reaches completion in Jesus Christ.

Jesus at the centre of the plan of salvation

In point of fact, Christ is at the heart of God's plan: "I am the Alpha and the Omega, the first and the last, the beginning and the end." (Rev 22 : 13.) The mystery of salvation finds its centre in him, as St Paul indicates in Ephesians: "Blessed be the God and Father of Our Lord Jesus Christ... he has chosen us in him before the foundation of the world, that we should be holy and blameless before him. He destined us in love to be his sons through Jesus Christ, according to the purpose of his will. In him we have redemption through his blood, the forgiveness of our trespasses, according to the riches of his grace which he lavished upon us. For he has made known to us in all wisdom and insight the mystery of his will, according to his purpose which he set forth in Christ as a plan for the fulness of time, to unite all things in him, things in heaven and things on earth." (Eph 1 : 3–10.)

Jesus, whose name means "Yahweh saves" (Mt 1 : 21), is the saviour of the world. He comes not only for the people of Israel, but for all mankind. That is the lesson of Christ's encounter with the Samaritan woman; after having spoken to her, Christ stayed two days with the Samaritans —heretics in Jewish eyes—and their response to him, which closes the episode, expresses its theological point: "We have heard for ourselves, and we know that this is indeed the Saviour of the world." (Jn 4 : 42.)

Nothing positive is effected in the order of salvation outside Christ, and those who have been and will be saved without knowing him have not been and will not be saved without his grace: "Apart from me you can do nothing." (Jn 15 : 5.)

It is also Christ who, making the salvation of mankind an achieved reality, brings about the return of everything in the universe to full harmony with God.

Finally, it is towards Christ's return that the expectation of the church is directed.

The person of Jesus

What makes Christianity different from any other religion is this very fact that the Christian finds salvation in a person, and that this person is the Son of God incarnate. To reduce Christianity to a set of doctrines, even very lofty ones, and forget him who is the Truth and the Life, would be to debase it completely. It must be the Christian's care "that some generalized idea does not gradually come to take the place of the Person of Christ."[1]

The gospel indicates at once his closeness, and his infinite dignity. Jesus appears throughout extremely human and very close to those among whom he lived: he takes part in the feasting at

[1] H. de Lubac, *The Splendour of the Church*, London 1956, 185.

the marriage of Cana, sits exhausted by Jacob's well and asks for a drink, weeps at Lazarus' tomb because Lazarus was his friend. He cares for individuals—the Samaritan woman and the rich young man, for instance. He is exquisitely aware of people: after raising Jairus' daughter, while everyone stood in stupefaction, it was he who asked them to give her something to eat. He is natural and welcoming to those who come to seek him—the blind men in Jericho, the messengers from John the Baptist, the children who are brought to him; he even answers the questions of those who want only to trap him.[1]

Yet in his bearing and his behaviour, Jesus created an impression of mystery on those around him. Glancing through Mark's Gospel, one is struck by the disciples' constant astonishment at him whom they felt so close and so great. They believed because they saw; the word he called them with was powerful; they were impressed by the authority with which he taught, and which made him so different from the scribes; the certainty with which he forgave sins, healed on the Sabbath day, and commanded the wind and the sea, gave them glimpses of his dignity as the Messiah, the son of God.[2] Similarly, St John who saw what place Judas' treason and the hour of his passion held in his Master's mind, and

---

[1] Jn 2 : 2; 4 : 6–7; 11 : 35; 4 : 7ff.; Mk 10 : 21; 5 : 43; Mt 20 : 29ff.; 11 : 2ff.; 19 : 13ff.; Lk 20 : 20ff.
[2] Mk 1 : 16ff.; 1 : 22; 2 : 1–12; 3 : 1–6; 4 : 35–41.

who related Jesus' distress to the thought of his coming death, also makes clear the sovereign liberty with which Christ accepted and fulfilled the will of his Father. Long beforehand, Jesus thought of the hour for which he had come, and knew who it was who would betray him, and the Johannine account of the passion stresses Christ's kingly freedom in his sacrifice.[1] Through all the sayings and doings of Jesus there could be seen glimpses of the mystery of his person, that of God's own Son made man.

To his disciples and the Jews who spoke with him—so imbued with the sense of Yahweh's transcendence and holiness—Jesus declared not only that he was the Messiah, but showed himself, by deed and word, as the Son of God. He revealed to them that he was himself God (Jn 10 : 30; 14 : 11), and died for having done so: "We have a law, and by that law he ought to die, because he has made himself the Son of God." (Jn 19 : 7.)

St John, summing up Christ's message and the faith of the early church on this point, wrote: "In the beginning was the Word, and the Word was with God, and the Word was God. . . . And the Word became flesh. . . . No one has ever seen God; the only Son, who is in the bosom of the Father, he has made him known." (Jn 1 : 1–14, 18.)

---

[1] Jn 6 : 70–1; 2 : 4; 12 : 27–8; 10 : 18; 13 : 1; 18 : 8; 18 : 33–7; 19 : 28–30.

The three phases of the mystery of Jesus
The incarnation

It is by design that after speaking of the eternal existence of the Word with the Father, and his work in creation, the evangelist uses the word "flesh" rather than "man" to express the reality of the incarnation. "Flesh" here does not mean the body as opposed to the soul, but rather in the well-known Semitic usage, man in the weak and sorry condition of his nature:

> All flesh is grass,
> > and all its beauty is like the flower of the field
> The grass withers, the flower fades,
> > when the breath of the Lord blows upon it.
> > [Is 40 : 6–7.]

It is quite legitimate, when thinking of the incarnation, to get lost in love and tenderness over the infant Christ lying in the manger; but one must not stop there: we must gaze with adult faith upon the mystery of God made man. Without ceasing to be God, the only begotten Son was made one of us: "He dwelt amongst us."

This closeness of God is the sign of love and of a call to a life of communion with him. But the objection may be raised: Christ remains as far from us as ever because he never sinned. (Heb 4 : 15; 2 Cor 5 : 21.) This however is a difficulty in appearance only: far from creating a gulf between Christ and ourselves, his infinite holiness makes him closer to those he has come to save. "All sin springs from a selfishness that shuts the heart in upon itself and lessens its power of sympathy", and Christ's holiness "only makes him the more our brother".[1]

If we except sin and "collusion between our flesh and sin",[2] then Christ shares our human condition totally. This shows that God does not despise the matter he has created, but wills to save all of man, not only his soul, but his body as well, and that he has in no way gone back on the original order of his creation as he willed it from the start. Christ has come not to save man by setting him free from matter, but by setting him free from sin; and the grace he pours out on the world comes not to destroy the order established by its Creator, but to sanctify the men living in it, and by that fact to re-establish all creation as God-orientated. The Christian notion of marriage, the manifestation of charity in concrete activities, the existence of a visible church, the setting up of the sacraments, these are a few of the many expressions of the principle contained in the fact of the incarnation. We find again the optimism of revelation about the created world—an optimism expressed from the first page of Genesis ("God saw that it was good"), and implied by belief in the resurrection.

---

[1] A. Médebielle, "Epître aux Hébreux", in *La Sainte Bible*, vol. 12, Paris 1946, 308.

[2] F. X. Durrwell, *The Resurrection*, London 1960, 47, n. 20. On the various senses of the word "flesh" in St Paul, see the *Bible de Jérusalem*'s comments on Rom 7 : 5.

The incarnation of the Son of God is an event written into time; it is God's entry into history to give it its deepest reality and meaning. In Jesus Christ history finds its true direction and its dynamism; it is he who makes it the history of salvation.

The passion

Christ in fact became man to save men. One with mankind, he died on the cross "to gather into one the children of God who are scattered abroad" (Jn 11 : 52) by sin, thus showing how faithful God is to his promises of salvation (Rom 3 : 21)[1] and to his love: "God shows his love for us in that while we were yet sinners, Christ died for us." (Rom 5 : 8.)

The perfect sacrifice, accomplished once and for all (Heb 7 : 27), his obedience unto death is the act of religion and love by which mankind, in the person of its head, returns to the Father and finds friendship with God once more; it is the supreme expression of Christ's love both for his Father and for mankind. For a better understanding of its significance, it is useful to consider some of the aspects under which Christ's sacrifice is presented in the New Testament.

Christ's sacrifice is the obedience of the new Adam bringing justification and an overflowing of grace where the disobedience of the first Adam had brought sin and death; solidarity in sin is

[1] The "righteousness of God" here means principally, though not only, God's faithfulness to his promises to save us.

replaced by solidarity in grace: "As by one man's disobedience many were made sinners, so by one man's obedience many will be made righteous." (Rom 5 : 19.)

Christ's sacrifice is also the sacrifice of the new covenant between God and men. Christ himself, the "mediator of the new covenant" (Heb 19 : 15) says: "This is my blood of the covenant, which is poured out for many for the forgiveness of sins." (Mt 26 : 28.) By his sacrifice, Christ has inaugurated the covenant foretold by the prophets, the new covenant establishing between God and man a union of life far more perfect than anything that could have been expected under the old.

Christ's sacrifice is also presented as the sacrifice of expiation, setting men free from sin, and uniting them with the life of God. This aspect, which we find in Hebrews and in Romans, is connected with the last. To understand it, we must relate it to the ritual of expiation. In the sacrifice of the covenant on Sinai, the spilling of the victims' blood both on the altar, which represented God, and on the people, signified that henceforth there would be a certain community of life between God and the people; but since Israel had promised to observe the law, the sin of the people went against the covenant, so each year they celebrated the feast of the expiation. On that day the High Priest, taking the blood of the sacrifice as a symbol of the life of the people, entered the Holy of Holies and sprinkled the mercy seat with blood. This, a massive gold plaque at the top of the ark of the covenant was the place of God's manifestation to Israel, and the rite signified the reconciliation of the people with God, and the reaffirming of the community of life established by the covenant between God and his people and endangered by sin. When St Paul wrote that "God put [Christ] forward as an expiation by his blood, to be received by faith" (Rom 3 : 25),[1] he meant that Christ's sacrifice was the decisive sacrifice of expiation liberating men from sin, and uniting them in a vital fashion with God.

Christ's sacrifice is also the sacrifice of the new Passover. This is supported by texts throughout the New Testament. "Christ, our paschal lamb, has been sacrificed", says St Paul (1 Cor 5 : 7), and St John, in his account of the passion, tells us the same thing. When the soldiers, having broken the legs of the two thieves, decided not to break Christ's because he was already dead, the evangelist comments: "These things took place that the scripture might be fulfilled, Not a bone of him shall be broken." (19 : 36.) By recalling these words, which referred to the paschal lamb (Ex 12 : 46)[2] at the very hour when the Jews were immolating the lambs for the Passover in the temple, a matter of yards from Calvary, St John clearly

[1] In the *Bible de Jérusalem*, Père Lyonnet gives the translation: "set him forth, the instrument of propitiation through his own blood"; see Lev 4 : 3–21; 16 : 1–34.

[2] There may also have been intended an allusion to the just man in Ps 34 : 21.

wanted to show that Jesus was the lamb of the new Passover, of the new exodus in which mankind passes from this world into the kingdom of the Father, and leaves the slavery of sin for the freedom of the children of God.

The resurrection

The paschal nature of Christ's sacrifice shows the dynamic continuity between Christ's death and his resurrection. It would be inadequate indeed to see the resurrection as no more than the reward for his heroic offering, or the sign of his being accepted by the Father. The final and glorious establishment of Christ at his Father's side is the natural conclusion of the total gift of himself that he made on the cross; the resurrection is the logical result of, and final seal on, his attitude of soul. And just as Christ on the cross acts not as an isolated individual, but as head of all humanity, so that his offering includes ours in essence, so his resurrection is that of the head of the whole human race, and constitutes the first fruits of ours: "Christ has been raised from the dead, the first fruits of those who have fallen asleep." (1 Cor 15 : 20.)

The resurrection is also the completion of Jesus' messianic career: risen in glory at the Father's right hand, established in his humanity in his full dignity as Lord and Messiah, Jesus, having offered his life on the cross, is given possession of the Spirit, and gives him to the world as had been promised for the messianic age. From Pentecost onwards (and Pentecost in Congar's words, is simply Easter with its fulfilment)[1] his role as Messiah is that of the Lord who sanctifies and is always helping the church with his Spirit: "Being exalted at the right hand of God, and having received from the Father the promise of the Holy Spirit, he has poured out this...." (Ac 2 : 33.)

It is to the risen Lord that Christians are united by grace from the moment of baptism, him to whom they pray, him whom they receive in the eucharist. It is the risen Lord, living now, who at every moment of history works upon the world by sending the Holy Spirit.

Christ, source of grace and truth

Having affirmed the fact of the incarnation, St John suggests at the end of his prologue the parallel between Moses, through whom the law was given, and Jesus, who communicates grace and truth to us: "The law was given through Moses: grace and truth came through Jesus Christ." (Jn 1 : 17.)

By bringing truth and life into the world, Christ responds to man's most fundamental religious aspirations—his desire to know God and share in his life. In the non-revealed religions we find remarkable efforts to attain to knowledge of God, and in the Old Testament we see Moses asking God to reveal his Name, asking to contemplate his glory. (Ex 3 : 13; 33 : 18.) Christ satisfies this need by revealing to man

[1] Y. Congar, *The Mystery of the Church*, 5.

what he could never discover by his own reason: the divine plan of salvation, which St Paul calls the mystery, and the fact that in the one and only God there are three Persons, distinct but equal, Father, Son and Holy Spirit. Though the mystery of the Trinity will always remain beyond human understanding, its revelation none the less throws great and unsuspected light on the inner life of God: "No one has ever seen God; the only Son, who is in the bosom of the Father, he has made him known." (Jn 1 : 18.)[1]

Christ also gives man the grace of being able to share in the divine life: "To all who received him ... he gave power to become children of God." (1 : 12.)

In working out the expressions of his aspirations to share God's life, man came up against a twofold obstacle: he could either affirm the existence of that communion at the risk of compromising the transcendent and personal nature of God, or reject the possibility of that communion in his anxiety to maintain the transcendence. The grace we receive from Christ's "fullness" (Jn 1 : 16) clearly does not make man a divine person—Jesus remains the only Son—but makes him a partaker in Christ's life as son, capable of reaching out towards God in the mystery of his inner life, a "son in the Son"[2]: "See what love the

[1] See textbooks of theology for the exact meaning of the word "person", and of the announcement of the mystery.
[2] The expression is from Mersch, *The Whole Christ*, London 1949.

Father has given us, that we should be called children of God; and so we are." (1 Jn 3 : 1.)

This life received from Christ transfigures man's religious life and his relationships with his neighbour; having become a "son in the Son", his attitude to the Father is that of a son, and he sees his neighbour as a brother in Christ, or at least as someone called to become so. Everything is made new by the fact that he has received from Christ the supernatural life which makes it possible to know and love God as Father, Son and Holy Spirit.

The new commandment

Christ's mission and work are the expression of God's love. The gift of truth and life to man makes it possible for him to respond to that love. Hence there is nothing surprising in the fact that Christ's command to his disciples is one of love. "A new commandment I give to you, that you love one another; even as I have loved you, that you also love one another. By this all men will know that you are my disciples, if you have love for one another." (Jn 13 : 34–5.)

Even in the Old Testament there was a precept of brotherly love: "You shall not hate your brother in your heart.... You shall not take vengeance or bear any grudge against the sons of your own people, but you shall love your neighbour as yourself; I am the Lord.... The stranger who sojourns with you shall be to you as the native among you, and you shall love him as yourself.... I am the Lord your God." (Lev 19: 17, 18, 34.)

The commandment of brotherly love given to the disciples is new in more ways than one. It is so because it constitutes the distinctive mark of the new covenant and of those who belong to it. The apostles followed Christ in stressing this capital point of Christian teaching very clearly. (cf. 1 Cor 13: and the epistles of John and James.) It is new also because it rests on a new principle—no longer only the love of Yahweh shown in bringing Israel out of Egypt, but the love of Christ even unto death, which became the basis of Christian charity. And finally, it is new because Christ carries it to a new perfection both in its object and its quality; the precept in Leviticus was concerned with Israelites and strangers living among them, whereas Christ's command is more absolute in its universalism, and is concerned with all mankind. And while the precept in Leviticus spoke of loving one's neighbour as oneself, Christ's command calls upon us to love our neighbour as Christ loves— in other words with a love that will not stop short of total self-sacrifice.

Such a precept leaves no room for any conscious acceptance of a life of mediocrity: "To the ancient world, Christendom revealed itself as love—and Christians of all ages must remain lovers or cease to be Christians."[1]

[1] W. Grossouw, *Revelation and Redemption: an Introduction to the Theology of St John*, London 1958, 41.

Our attitude towards Christ

At the end of his gospel, St John indicates in a few words what his object was in writing it: "Jesus did many other signs in the presence of the disciples, which are not written in this book; but these are written that you may believe that Jesus is the Christ, the Son of God, and that believing you may have life in his name." (Jn 20 : 30–1.)

The essence of man's attitude to Christ is faith. To say this in no way contradicts what has been said earlier about charity, for the faith involved here includes charity. In the presence of the incarnate Word, it marks the line of demarcation between those who knowingly refuse to believe in him and those who, helped by grace, but still fully free, accept his testimony, believe in him, and are given life: "He came to his own home, and his own people received him not. But to all who received him, who believed in his name, he gave power to become children of God." (Jn 1 : 11–12.)

The faith St John speaks of is faith in a person, the person of Christ: this explains the place of the person of Christ in the life of a Christian. This faith is also a receiving of the word God speaks in his Son, which explains the importance for believers of knowing the gospel, and of living their whole spiritual life in the light of Christ's message and mystery (incarnation-passion-resurrection). It is also faith filled with hope: "In the world you have tribulation; but be of good cheer, I have overcome the world." (Jn 16 : 33.) Finally, it is a faith which involves the acceptance of God's will as expressed in the word and message of Christ: without this aspect of commitment, faith would not be wholly sincere; "to receive Christ" means to adopt towards him a religious attitude engaging one's whole person and whole life. Faith, in the Johannine and Pauline sense, must of necessity be accompanied by charity. "True faith, genuine faith, brings with it complete surrender of the entire personality to the person of Christ."[1]

Reading

Jn 1 : 1–18; Eph 1 : 3–19; Phil 2 : 6–11; 1 Cor 1 : 17 – 2 : 9; Rom 5 : 1–21; Ac 2 : 14–36; 1 Jn 3 : 1–2; Rom 8

[1] Grossouw, 114–15.

12

The Church

The church in the continuity of salvation history

The church fits into the development of the plan of salvation just as the people of the new covenant succeed the people of the old. St Paul unhesitatingly describes Abraham, father of the chosen people, as father of Christians, whether or not they are his descendants physically: "And if you are Christ's, then you are Abraham's offspring, heirs according to promise." (Gal 3 : 29.)

The Christian people are called by St Paul "the Israel of God" (Gal 6 : 16), and St Peter writes to the Christian communities in terms taken from the Old Testament: "You are a chosen race, a royal priesthood, a holy nation, God's own people, that you may declare the wonderful deeds of him who called you out of darkness into his marvellous light. Once you were no people, but now you are God's people." (1 Pt 2 : 9–10.)

The continuity between the people of the new covenant and the people of Israel is expressed even in the vocabulary used in the New Testament. The expression "church of God" meant, in the Old Testament, the assembly (*ekklesia* in Septuagint Greek) of the Israelites gathered by Moses at Yahweh's command, and the "day of the Assembly" meant the day when the sacred assembly received the law on Sinai (Dt 18 : 16)[1]; when St Paul speaks of "the church of God which is at Corinth", or, in the epistles of the captivity, of "the church", he is transferring to the Christian community expressions which used to designate Israel, so as to make clear that this is the new people of God. When Christ speaks of "his church" it is, of course, to distinguish it from the people of the old covenant, but also to show that the people of the new covenant follow on the heels of those of the old in the unfolding of the history of salvation.

In this connection, we must say of the church what we said earlier of Christ's work: it is at once in continuity and in discontinuity with the Old Testament, since Christ perfected the law in a higher reality. The church is the people of the new covenant, prefigured historically by the people of the old covenant; but it is not the people of God in the sense "that it inherited the legal status of the former people of God, or could be added or partially assimilated to it."[2]

The election of Israel as depository of the promises and of revelation was realised with Christ and the church in mind, as it were, and its very nature was the sign that it could be no

[1] See Cerfaux, *The Church in the Theology of St Paul*, London 1959.
[2] A. Chavasse, "Du peuple de Dieu à l'Eglise du Christ", *La Maison-Dieu*, 32, 49.

more than provisional, no more than the preparation for a more universal and more perfect reality. The church is not bound up with one special people, but is universal: "Instead of being the raising up of a single human group, like the former people of God, it transcends them all without exception."[1] "There is neither Jew nor Greek, there is neither slave nor free, there is neither male nor female; for you are all one in Christ Jesus." (Gal 3 : 28.)

The detailed forms of the law have disappeared, being fulfilled in a more perfect reality, and thus having lost their purpose—this is clear from the way the dispute between the Judaising Christians and those who came from paganism was settled in St Paul's time. The church, unlike the people of Israel, is not waiting for the promises to be fulfilled; though she awaits the Lord's return, she already possesses the reality of salvation in its essence. From this point of view, we may say that the religion of expectation has been succeeded by the religion of possession.[2] Finally, unlike the religious institution of the Israelites, the church as Christ's body is itself the means of union with God, and the place where it takes place: "We are faced with an entirely fresh metaphysical notion of what religion is. In the old covenant, formal religion was not the instrument and actual point of union with God. It signified a union to come, and only worked to bring it about in anticipa-

[1] Chavasse, 52.
[2] Chavasse, 46–8.

tion by the fact of the announcement it made of it. Now it is the religious institution that of itself brings about union with God."[1]

Christ and the church

In other words, between Christ and the church there exists not merely continuity, but extension, a living union.

The church was founded by Christ: "You are Peter, and on this rock I will build my church." (Mt 16 : 18.)

It was Christ who chose the disciples and apostles, who trained them and sent them into the world, who gave them the Holy Spirit.

And it is Christ from whom the church has received the promise of eternal life. Jesus' final words in Matthew bear witness to this: "Lo, I am with you always, to the close of the age." (28 : 20.)

This does not mean that the church cannot experience a failure or a reverse, at one or another point of the globe, at one or another moment of history; but Christians, whether during the first persecutions, or in the world today, find in these words of Christ an extraordinary assurance; and the message of the Book of Revelation is designed to remind those who suffer for their faith that Christ has promised eternity to his church: "The powers of death shall not prevail against it." (Mt 16 : 18.)

[1] Chavasse, 48.

Furthermore, it is faith in Christ that holds the church together in unity: we enter it by being baptised "in the name of the Lord Jesus". (Ac 19 : 5.) Just as belief in Yahweh was the distinguishing mark and unity of the Israelites, so belief in Jesus as Lord is the distinguishing mark and unity of Christians. St Paul, writing to the Corinthians, extends the wish that he formulates at the beginning of the letter to "all those who in every place call on the name of our Lord Jesus Christ". (1 Cor 1 : 2.)

Baptism, the sacrament of faith, is a new birth. Drawn together in faith in the Lord Jesus, the church lives by Christ and in him. In this connection, one must never forget the importance Christ attached to the eucharist, *the* sacrament above all others, to which baptism is itself orientated, and by which our Saviour continues to give life to the church: "Truly, truly I say to you, unless you eat the flesh of the Son of man and drink his blood, you have no life in you; he who eats my flesh and drinks my blood has eternal life and I will raise him up at the last day.... As the living Father sent me, and I live because of the Father, he who eats me will live because of me." (Jn 6 : 53–7.)

The reality of the living union between Christ and the church is expressed by Jesus in the allegory of the vine, and by St Paul in his words about the church as the Body of Christ.

The people of Israel was the vine of whom Isaiah spoke at the beginning of his ministry (Is 5 : 1–7; it is a theme found in several of the prophets, and even today is used on some of the coins of Israel); the new people of God is the true vine that draws life from its union with Christ; this is clear from the discourse after the last supper, when Jesus speaks of himself as the true vine in which one must remain if one is to bear fruit: "I am the true vine.... As the branch cannot bear fruit by itself, unless it abides in the vine, neither can you, unless you abide in me. I am the vine, you are the branches. He who abides in me, and I in him, he it is that bears much fruit, for apart from me you can do nothing." (Jn 15 : 1–5.)

When he embarks on the theme of the church as body of Christ, St Paul insists both on the close union of Christians with Christ, and their solidarity as a result (1 Cor 7 : 12ff.) and on the influx of life which Christ, the "Head", communicates to the church: "We are to grow up in every way into him who is the head, into Christ, from whom the whole body, joined and knit together by every joint with which it is supplied, when each part is working properly, makes bodily growth and upbuilds itself in love." (Eph 4 : 15–16.) In speaking of the church as the bride of Christ, Paul stresses more the church's union and submission in love to him who is at once the "Saviour of the Body" and its Head. (Eph 5 : 22–32.)

This union of Christ and the church makes possible a better understanding of the church's place in God's plan: the very existence of the church is bound up with the incarnation, the mystery of God becoming man and entering human history to save mankind. The union of the church with the incarnate Word, the transmission of the gospel by men, its written expression in the inspired books of the New Testament, the existence of the sacraments—gestures that signify and contain Christ's grace (baptism is "the washing of water with the word" in Eph. 5 : 26)—the establishment of a liturgy around the "breaking of bread" (Ac 2 : 42), the designation of the apostles and of heads of churches analogous to the organisation of other human societies; all this does not reduce the church to a purely human society, but shows us her place in the development of the incarnation.

The Spirit and the church

In the Old Testament, the outpouring of the Spirit had been promised for the messianic era; Peter recalled this in his discourse at Pentecost, quoting a passage from Joel in which the universal outpouring of the Spirit is predicted. (Ac 2 : 16–21; Jl 2 : 28–9.) In his discourse after the last supper, and again before the ascension, Jesus himself had promised the apostles the gift of the Holy Spirit: "John baptised with water, but before many days you shall be baptised with the Holy Spirit." (Ac 1 : 5.)

Dead, risen, glorified at the right hand of the Father, Christ completed his messianic role on the day of Pentecost, by pouring out upon his church the Holy Spirit he had promised. This, the fulfilment of Easter, the mystery of Pentecost, which continues as long as the church exists, is the final Christological mystery before the return of Christ. In a theophany which was at once her "baptism", the bestowal of the law whereby she lives, and the opening of her mission, the church solemnly received the Holy Spirit. This gift was for her a decisive event, for it marked definitively her religious status: the Spirit Christ communicated to his church is her light, her life and her strength.

The Spirit enlightens the church by making her aware of the wealth of revelation Christ has given her. In his discourse after the last supper Jesus said to his apostles: "These things I have spoken to you while I am still with you. But the Counsellor, the Holy Spirit, whom the Father will send in my name, he will teach you all things, and bring to your remembrance all that I have said to you." (Jn 14 : 25–6.) The Holy Spirit given at Pentecost enlightened the church. Some of the things the Lord said and did were not understood by the apostles until then,[1] and the New Testament gives evidence of their ever-deepening grasp of Christ's message under the guidance of the Holy Spirit. Revelation ended with the apostolic age, but the Spirit continues to enlighten the church. By his light she still

---

[1] The sign of the temple, Jn 2 : 22; the triumphal entry into Jerusalem, Jn 12 : 16.

studies Christ's message, exploring all its aspects, all its possibilities, living it, announcing it to the world, and making it the object of her contemplation and her meditative faith. Tradition is not the discovery of new truths, but the transmission, ever more perfectly expressed, of the riches of revelation.

The Spirit sanctifies the church and gives her life. He dwells in her as in a temple. (1 Cor 3 : 16.) He directs and inspires the prayer of Christians to the Father: "God has sent the Spirit of his Son into our hearts, crying, Abba, Father!" (Gal 4 : 6.) "The Spirit helps us in our weakness; for we do not know how to pray as we ought, but the Spirit himself intercedes for us with sighs too deep for words." (Rom 8 : 26.) Together with the Father and the Son, he shares out spiritual gifts and vocations in the church: "There are varieties of gifts, but the same Spirit. ... All these are inspired by one and the same Spirit, who apportions to each one individually as he wills." (1 Cor 12 : 4, 11.)

Despite the sense generally given today to the word *charism*, it is noteworthy that, in the lists of spiritual gifts that we find in the Pauline epistles,[1] ministries which have nothing of the miraculous about them (apostles, pastors, doctors, tasks of governing, helping the less fortunate etc.) are mentioned alongside more extraordinary and mystical gifts. There is then no reason to oppose "charisms" to ecclesial func-

[1] Cor 12 : 8–10, 28–30; Rom 12 : 6–8; Eph 4 : 11–12.

tions: both are gifts of the Spirit. In this connection it is useful to note that Christ sends the Spirit to the church he instituted as such; one must therefore take care not to see the sanctifying Spirit in opposition either to the intelligible content of Christ's message, or to all that is institutional in the church Christ founded: "Now, if the Holy Spirit is really at work, and if it is wrong to make for the Church as institution claims so exclusive, so purely legalistic, as to leave no room for the action of the Spirit, it would be an error at least as great, and certainly more dangerous, to appeal to the Holy Spirit and to expect everything directly from him, while ignoring the positive datum derived from Christ's institution, which it is precisely the mission of the Spirit to make real and actual in us."[1]

The Holy Spirit bears the church forward to witness to Christ, and sustains her in that witness. Before he left this world, Jesus had said to the apostles: "You shall receive power when the Holy Spirit has come upon you; and you shall be my witness in Jerusalem and in all Judaea and Samaria, and to the ends of the earth." (Ac 1 : 8.) The incidents recounted in Acts show the missionary dynamism that the Holy Spirit at every instant communicated to the church, and the strength he gave her in persecution, just as Jesus had foretold: "When they deliver you up, do not be anxious how you are to speak or what you are to say; for what you are to say will be

[1] Y. Congar, *The Mystery of the Church*, 17.

given to you in that hour; for it is not you who speak, but the Spirit of your Father speaking through you." (Mt 10 : 19–20.)

Even today the Spirit raises up missionaries and apostles in the church, and supports Christians in their witness. A Chinese student was asked not long ago to explain his faith and answered thus: "Our secret organisation is the Holy Spirit. In Manchuria, Africa, America, Europe, and here, Catholics everywhere believe and say the same thing because it is the same Spirit who dwells in our hearts and speaks through our mouths. It is he who puts into my mouth what I am saying to you, and that is why I am saying the same thing as Catholics all over the world."

The church's mission

The church's mission prolongs that of Christ, who came to bring truth and life to the world: it is to incorporate mankind more and more into the risen Christ by communicating to them the life and truth she gets from her Head. Because she is Christ's body, the church does not hand these gifts on as external realities transmitted from without—she herself is the place where communion with Christ in truth and life is realised.

The church has been charged by Christ to announce the gospel to the world. As he left the eleven, Christ said to them: "Go into all the world and preach the gospel to the whole creation." (Mk 16 : 14.)

Writing to the Ephesians, St Paul declares that he has been chosen "to preach to the Gentiles the unsearchable riches of Christ, and to make all men see what is the plan of the mystery hidden for ages in God who created all things; that through the church the manifold wisdom of God might now be made known to the principalities and powers in the heavenly places. This was according to the eternal purpose which he has realised in Christ Jesus." (Eph 3 : 8–11.)

As "the official machinery through which God promulgates the Gospel to the world",[1] the church fulfils her mission in proclaiming that gospel. We know how important the word is in the Acts, and how deeply aware Paul was of his responsibility towards the gospel he had received: "If I preach the gospel, that gives me no ground for boasting. For necessity is laid upon me. Woe to me if I do not preach the gospel!" (1 Cor 9 : 16.) In the same vein, he tells Timothy: "I charge you in the presence of God and of Christ Jesus ... preach the word, be urgent in season and out of season, convince, rebuke and exhort, be unfailing in patience and in teaching." (2 Tim 4 : 1–2.)

All the New Testament writings show how the message was handed on by the early church. "There is ... one Lord, one faith, one baptism", declares St Paul (Eph 4 : 5), and he warns the

[1] Daniélou, *The Lord of History*, 283.

Galatians, faced with the intrigues of the Judaisers, "Even if we, or an angel from heaven, should preach to you a gospel contrary to that which we preached to you, let him be accursed!" (1 : 8.)

The church knows herself responsible for proclaiming Christ's message, and knows also that she has no right to alter it. She would rather incur the reproach of being intransigent or opportunist than show herself unfaithful to her mission by adapting the faith and morals of the gospel to any form of selfishness.

The church's announcing of the gospel takes place not only through preaching; the life of the church is also in its way a proclaiming of the message. Charity is the sign which marks Christians as Christ's disciples, and their unity is a sign to the world that Christ has indeed sent them and that he loves them: "... that they may become perfectly one, so that the world may know that thou hast sent me and hast loved them even as thou hast loved me." (Jn 17 : 23.)

The church also has the mission to communicate to men the supernatural life: "Make disciples of all nations, baptising them in the name of the Father and of the Son and of the Holy Spirit, teaching them to observe all that I have commanded you." (Mt 28 : 19–20.)

The church transmits the life of Christ, and draws all men reborn by baptism towards sanctity: the sacraments, liturgical prayer and pastoral formation in charity all combine, in their different ways, towards that work of sanctification whereby man gradually moves from the old world to the new. The church communicates the supernatural life because she is the body whose head is Christ, and there is no distinguishing life in Christ from life in the church. The baptism that unites us to Christ incorporates us at the same time into the church: "For by one spirit we were all baptised into one body." (1 Cor 12 : 13.) The eucharist which unites us to Christ brings about the unity of the church: "Because there is one bread, we who are many are one body, for we all partake of the same bread." (1 Cor 10 : 17.) In this way, each of the sacraments communicates the life of Christ, and incorporates us more fully into that church which, because he is her Head, mediates life and holiness.

It is to help the church to fulfil this mission of evangelising and sanctifying that Christ has given her a hierarchy and assists them infallibly. He himself chose the apostles, and set them up as the pastors of his church, promising and then giving Peter the primacy among them. The history of the early communities show how important Peter and the apostles were in the life of the early church, and apart from a few privileges special to the apostles, the hierarchy is the same today—in the person of the pope, and in the college of bishops, with their threefold power of magisterium, government, and order. The establishment of the hierarchy gives pope and bishops special powers and responsibilities as regards evangelising, pastoral work and worship, but does not therefore exclude the other members of the church from the mission she holds from Christ. Each man, in his own sphere, is called to work together with the pastors for the announcing of the gospel, and the sanctification of the world by Christ.[1]

[1] It is worthwhile to explain how the pope and bishops are the legitimate successors of Peter and the apostles. To do this one must study in detail the texts concerning Jesus' promise to Peter (Mt 16 : 13–20), and his primacy (Lk 22 : 31; Jn 21 : 15–17), and those dealing with Christ's establishing the apostles, giving them their mission, and promising the assistance of the Holy Spirit to the church. It must also be shown how the church worked out in practice the hierarchical institution given her by Christ: the importance of Peter and the apostles in the Acts and the epistles, and the changeover from communities governed by a council of elders, under the supervision of the apostles, to communities each governed by its own ruling bishop, as we find at the time of St Ignatius of Antioch (the pastoral epistles reflect this period of transition which coincided with the death of the apostles). It must, finally, be shown how the church, under the guidance of the Holy Spirit, understood from the first that the promises and commands given directly to the apostles and Peter by Christ were intended to outlive their human lifetime, and were in fact a setting up, in their persons, of a permanent hierarchy that was to last as long as the church's pilgrimage in the world. The limits imposed on a study such as this make it impossible to give the necessary theological working-out of all this, but it can be found in works of theology concerned with the church. For a serious, though preliminary, total view of all this, see P. A. Liégé. "Le Mystère de l'Eglise" in *Initiation théologique*, vol. 4, 2nd ed., Paris 1956. This book (or any good study of the church) will also show precisely the foundation, purpose, conditions, and limitations of infallibility in the church.

Aspects of the church

If the church has such a place in God's plan and so important a mission in the world, if she is indissolubly united to Christ and animated by the Holy Spirit, how is it that she is so often a scandal or incomprehensible to our contemporaries? Such reactions are most frequent among those who judge the church from outside and as a purely human institution instead of the mystery she is, or those who have failed to grasp one or another aspect of her living complexity.

There is no lack of historical, exegetical and rational justifications for the church, and Christians should know what they are, but the church is not a problem to be solved: she is a living mystery to be known only from within. Like the mystery of salvation of which she is part, the church becomes more comprehensible in proportion to our becoming more mature in Christ, and more deeply rooted in charity: "The church is fully comprehensible only for those who see things with her eyes, for those, ultimately, who live in her."[1]

What often shocks the unbeliever when he meets the church, is the imperfections and sins he finds among Christians. Holy with the holiness of Christ who gives her grace, holy in the sacraments she administers and the word she transmits, holy by the efforts and fruits of holi-

[1] Y. Congar, *The Mystery of the Church*, London 1960.

ness produced in her by the Holy Spirit, the church in the world is made up of men reborn by baptism, yet still subject to sin, and obliged to struggle unceasingly if they are to remain faithful to Christ: they are justified, but not impeccable. To say this is no kind of justification for a Christian being resigned to his own mediocrity, but it must be remembered when we look at the church as a whole. To lament that all Christians are not saints, or that the church's work in the world is no further forward after twenty centuries of Christianity, is legitimate insofar as the reason lies in personal sins and omissions. But the way such lamentations are expressed sometimes amounts to forgetting the concrete conditions in which Christian life must unfold, and the fact that the battle starts afresh with every man (on the situation of the justified Christian, see Rom 6).

The church, in short, is not simply an inheritance from the past, but an actual, living, dynamic reality: she is the body of Christ now living and growing. Whoever enters that body by baptism can never settle down to do nothing in it, because he belongs to that body which "upbuilds itself in love" (Eph 4 : 16), to the people of God journeying towards the new land of promise (see 1 Cor 10: 1–11), he is involved in that building and that journeying, and has a share of responsibility in the whole. With the whole brotherly community of those who live in Christ, he must do his best to respond in faith and love to the call he has heard to "build up the Body of Christ, until we all attain to the unity of the faith and of the knowledge of the Son of God, to mature manhood, to the measure of the stature of the fullness of Christ". (Eph 4 : 12–13.)

The eschatological nature of the church does not, however, make the Christian a stranger to the human community. If the church is not "of the world" in the Johannine sense (the *world* here being seen in opposition to God), she remains in it: "They are not of the world, even as I am not of the world. I do not pray that thou shouldst take them out of the world, but that thou shouldst keep them from evil." (Jn 17 : 14–15.)

Christ's kingdom is not of this world, but this does not mean that those in the church can dissociate themselves from the human community: the order of Creation as willed by God, the divine intention to restore all things in Christ, and the charity that will be the yardstick whereby we are judged, requires us to fulfil our human tasks in faithfulness to the gospel —with all that those tasks involve in the way of civic, social and family duties. His hope of a heavenly city does not take the Christian out of the world God has placed him in; the more worthy he is to be called a Christian, the more valuable a member of the human community he will be[1]: to think of religion as "the opium of

[1] The sacrifice of some of this world's claims for priestly or contemplative vocations is justifiable—even from the human standpoint—because such vocations

the people" is to demonstrate a total misunderstanding of what charity and Christianity are.

The attitude of the Christian in the church

The Christian's first attitude towards the mystery of the church is one of faith. It is in her that God shows his fidelity to his promises of salvation, in her that Christ gathers all mankind together into himself. Faced with God's plan, it is not for the Christian to choose the means by which God effects salvation, but to accept freely the plan God has chosen. Rather than rest content with a superficial, and thus inexact, picture of the church, he tries to know her better, by studying revelation and the teaching of the hierarchy. He attaches great importance to unity of faith, and tries to understand the church from within by living that faith. It is Christ he obeys through the directives and orders of those whose mission is to govern, and he can make his own Newman's prayer:

> May I never forget for a moment that thou hast established on earth a kingdom that belongs to thee, that the church is thy work... that when the church speaks it is thou who speakest... may the weakness of thy human representatives never lead me to forget that it

---

are a living witness to the community of spiritual realities; they are a witness it needs, not only to discourage its members from limiting their aspirations to the city of this world, but also to give them and their temporal affairs a total human equilibrium.

is thou that speakest and workest through them.

This attitude of faith leads Christians to a sense of belonging to the church. Aware of belonging to the fraternal community, they do not act in isolation, but sense a solidarity with all their brothers in Christ. In the liturgy, in the eucharist in particular, individualism is forgotten, and we express by our actions and attitudes the communion of all in Christ and his sacrifice. Following the church's life in the world, every Christian knows that he is to some extent responsible for that life and its message, and he seeks in the apostolate not personal success, but to fulfil his mission in regard to the building up of the body of Christ. Seeing the failures of some or other of his brothers in the faith, he does not judge the church from outside or as a pharisee, but suffers with her: "As long as you accept the feeling that you are personally concerned by everything that is part of the Church, even by a word of one of her priests..., that means you are trusting her. It isn't suffering we should be afraid of, but detachment. We mustn't ever cut ourselves off! Suffering *because* of the Church is nothing: we've got to suffer *in* the Church."[1] Every Christian knows the frailty of human nature, and the sins and failings he sees do not scandalise him: they are rather a call to greater

---

[1] P. A. Lesort, *The Wind Bloweth where it Listeth*, London 1955, 308.

fidelity and more fraternal charity. The reaction of a Chinese student to the defection from the faith of a girl student in prison presents a perfect expression of this Catholic solidarity: "They have captured the heart of our sister, and we grieve, but do not think we are defeated. By beseeching Christ from the bottom of our suffering hearts, we have discovered our own weakness. Having resisted for over a year in complete isolation, our sister has fallen. We are all together in this vast struggle against the darkness that is trying to enfold us: if one falls, it is because the others have not helped him enough. We have not prayed or sacrificed ourselves enough. Only God can save us, and if we think we can attribute any merit to ourselves for not having fallen, then we are very close to losing the divine grace that is our only support."[1]

Accepting God's plan for the world in faith, knowing that one belongs to the church and actively living in communion with her—all this is normally accompanied by a humble sense of security in Christ, by joy in fulfilling God's will, and by gratitude to the Father who has "transferred us to the kingdom of his beloved Son". (Col 1 : 13.)

Reading

Mt 16: 13–20; 28: 16–20; Ac 1: 4–8; 2: 1–47; Mk 3: 13–19; 1 Cor 12: 4–30; Jn 15: 1–8; 16: 5–15; 17; 21: 15–17; Eph 1: 19 – 4: 16; 5: 22–33

[1] Helped by the prayers and love of her friends, the girl in fact soon returned to the faith.

13

The salvation of Jews and pagans

The problems

The salvation of non-Christians has always been a preoccupation of the church, which was sent by Christ to preach the gospel to the world. Having recognised Jesus as the one Saviour, and spurred on by true charity, Christians quickly began wondering about the eternal destiny of their friends and relations who remained pagans. Since the days of the apostles, new countries have been discovered which have brought this question to the forefront of our theological thinking, and indeed the scope of the problem has never been wider than in our day—now that science also shows that man's arrival on earth goes back a great deal further than Abraham. The nature of the problem is not changed by our more precise knowledge of the age of the world, but it does make it seem more important and more acute. What is the situation in regard to salvation of those millions of men who lived before Christ, or who have lived since but never really been told about him?

Another question which was very important to those first converted from Judaism was that of the salvation of the Jews. The chosen people as a whole neither recognised Christ nor accepted the church. The Jews who recognised Christ as the Messiah promised to Israel suffered intensely at the thought of those they loved remaining in the Jewish religion, and of their nation remaining outside the way of salvation at the moment when the promises were being fulfilled. In Romans, St Paul makes no secret of the pain it causes him: "I am speaking the truth in Christ, I am not lying; my conscience bears me witness in the Holy Spirit, that I have great sorrow and unceasing anguish in my heart. For I could wish that I myself were accursed and cut off from Christ for the sake of my brethren, my kinsmen by race." (9 : 1–3.)

Since then the problem of the salvation of the Jews has never been out of the church's mind. Though Christians living in contact with Jewish religious groups feel it most strongly, it is present in the prayer of the universal church. Today, the existence of Israel as a state, though not altering the religious facts, is psychologically a great help towards making Christians all over the world aware of the problems of the salvation of the children of Abraham.

Both these problems call for long and detailed study. In these few pages, I shall merely indicate a few basic principles that apply to both, and sketch some general lines along which a solution may lie.

The principles

Before saying anything further, it is worth pondering a comment made by Père Liégé about the many people who are to all appearances excluded from the requirements of salvation, though they have not themselves rejected them: "The word of God has little to tell us about their position. The magisterium makes no positive statement, merely keeping the principles contained in revelation intact, and rejecting any synthesis that disregards them. It falls to theology to work out a synthesis that is faithful to all the requirements of the word of God.... The results will always be unsatisfactory, for who knows the ways of God's mercy? They surpass all theology."[1]

The mystery of salvation as revealed by God in the bible is a plan of universal salvation to be brought about by Christ through membership in his body which is the church.

The dynamism of bible history, from the creation onwards, is directed towards the universal establishment of the kingdom of God, towards the heavenly Jerusalem described in Revelation. The Genesis traditions of Abel and Noah, the universal message of a book like Jonah, the whole history of Israel before Christ, all show the universality in both time and space of God's saving will. St Paul expresses it thus: "God our Saviour ... desires all men to be saved and to come to the knowledge of the truth." (1 Tim 2 :

[1] P.-A. Liégé, OP, "Le salut des 'autres'", in *Lumière et Vie*, 18, 14.

3–4.) It is clear, then, that the work of salvation is not limited by the chronological and geographical framework of Christ's coming and the preaching of the gospel. God's universal will to save means that he gives everyone the means necessary to salvation, and no one is damaged without deserving to be.

The bible makes it no less clear that Christ is the one and only Saviour. He is the Saviour of the world, and St Paul declares: "There is one God, and there is one mediator between God and men, the man Christ Jesus, who gave himself as a ransom for all." (1 Tim 2 : 5–6.) Every person who is saved, whether or not he knows Christ, and whatever his period of history, is saved by a grace from Christ.

It is clear too, that in God's plan no one is saved without belonging in some way to the church. For the church is not merely something founded by Christ at a given moment in history, but is also the "body of Christ"; therefore no one can receive sanctifying grace or live by Christ's life without in some sense being united to that body. Note, finally, that when Paul, in Ephesians, speaks of the completing of God's plan, the church he sees united to its head in glory is made up of all the saved. Therefore no one is saved without belonging to the church. In the case of the non-evangelised, that belonging can only be implicit: it will be included in a man's general disposition to cooperate with the order and means of salvation chosen by God, and in relation to the grace received from the fact of the mystery of Christ and his church.

But one must not therefore conclude that such an implicit membership is the normal rule, or that it can be enough in every case. Our Lord's words are quite definite: "Preach the gospel to the whole creation. He who believes and is baptised will be saved; but he who does not believe will be condemned." (Mk 16 : 15–16.)

Anyone who has *truly* seen the light of the gospel must belong explicitly and visibly to Christ and the church if he is to be saved; and it is the Lord's expressed will that the church should try visibly to incorporate as many men as possible. Since Christ's coming, any purely invisible union with the visible church has been an abnormal condition for salvation, and can only be sufficient for those who are held back from him and from the church he founded by invincible ignorance.

The bible also shows beyond all doubt the necessity for a religious attitude of faith if one is to be saved. It is not enough to have a rational knowledge of God, to concede from a philosophical point of view that God exists. There must be faith: "Without faith it is impossible to please him." (Heb 11 : 6.) The actual formulation of that faith may vary in explicitness in different cases, its concrete realisation be more or less developed, but the same religious disposition remains necessary in essence if man is to be saved.

The salvation of the non-evangelised

When it comes to the religious situation of people who have not been reached by positive revelation, we find, from reading the bible, that God makes them realise his providence towards them (and therefore his existence and his wisdom) through his works and his goodness: "In past generations he allowed all the nations to walk in their own ways; yet he did not leave himself without witness, for he did good and gave you from heaven rains and fruitful seasons, satisfying your hearts with food and gladness." (Ac 14 : 16–17.)

This evidence of God, and the inner thanksgiving that goes with it, show the world in a light that is not that of reason alone. The revelation of God through his works does not lead man merely to a philosophical conclusion that God exists. It manifests the living God who wills man's happiness, and it normally results in the religious attitude that St Paul reproaches the pagans of his day for not having adopted: "What can be known about God is plain to them, because God has always shown it to them. Ever since the creation of the world his invisible nature, namely his eternal power and deity, has been clearly perceived in the things that have been made. So they are without excuse; for although they knew God they did not honour him as God or give thanks to him...." (Rom 1 : 19–21.)

The saving attitude for man to adopt in response to God's revelation is faith—the religious adherence to the message addressed to him by God through his works; it is an attitude, furthermore, which involves the disposition to receive God's word should it come to his knowledge. The author of the epistle to the Hebrews makes the object of that faith clearer: "Whoever would draw near to God must believe that he exists and that he rewards those who seek him." (11 : 6.)

God exists and watches over man's salvation: "For every man, in whatever time or place he lives, faith in these two basic propositions is absolutely necessary to salvation."[1] Does this mean, then, that these articles of faith, which would be a quite inadequate confession of faith for a Christian, must of necessity be professed as explicitly as this by every man not possessed of positive revelation? In view of the religious state of the world today, theologians are wondering whether, for people educated and living in completely atheist surroundings, faith in these two propositions, though still necessary, might not be formulated less explicitly; whether it might not sometimes be realised and contained in embryo in the man who (with the help of grace) decides of set purpose to lead his life in unselfishness and does so, in continual reference to moral standards which he considers as absolute, and one might say, sacred, especially when

[1] Liégé, "Le salut des 'autres'", 20–21. See also in this connection the interesting article by Yves Congar OP, "Au sujet du salut des non-catholiques" in the *Revue des Sciences Religieuses*, Jan. 1958, 53–65.

his behaviour to his fellow man is truly brotherly. A man who is obedient and faithful to those moral values, though not fully aware of what he is doing, or that the Holy Spirit is guiding him, is in fact being obedient and faithful to God—for he is the Absolute, he is the foundation and the goal of every moral life. And this freely chosen conduct would produce the vital beginning of an attitude of faith capable of becoming some day more explicit. Provided, first, that one is careful to apply this only to an attitude of high moral stature, and not to just any form of altruism,[1] and second, that one remembers that this is only a hypothesis, lacking the precisions and shadings a theologian would give it,[2] this explanation appears to open a per-

[1] As Jean Daniélou has pointed out, "we find today an altruism that is not Christian, and even that is in some cases positively anti-Christian. Of course there are many cases where altruism can be most Christian, and some in which there is an evangelical spirit unaware of itself. But altruism can be completely and consciously anti-Christian, a supreme expression of modern man's claim that he does not need God, even to do good." ("L'esprit des Béatitudes dans la vie d'un militant ouvrier", in *Masses Ouvrières*, Nov. 1955, 41.) Obviously no altruism that really works on the principle that man can do without God can have anything in common with the attitude of faith.

[2] See this question treated by Liégé, "Le salut des 'autres'", 23–8 or *Initiation théologique*, vol. 4, 372–5, and vol. 3, 506–9. Of interest also is J. Mouroux's *I Believe*, London 1959. On p. 75, n. 1, the author quotes Maritain: "Under many names, names which are not that of God, in ways only known to God, the interior act of a soul's thought can be directed towards a reality

spective of theological thinking that is both interesting and healthily optimistic in regard to the salvation of the non-evangelised.

The faith of the non-evangelised is generally expressed in the religion they practise, which must be seen in relation to non-revealed religions as a whole. These up till the time of Christ were, outside Israel, the normal expression of man's religious impulses, though they played only a kind of caretaker role, filling in time till evangelisation should happen. Despite the hesitancy and the sometimes serious imperfections in their actual structures, these religions, because of the element of truth they expressed and the support they gave society were often of assistance to the life of faith.

The faith of the non-evangelised is not without its repercussions in their lives: it is a religious recognition of God and his saving providence, coupled with trust, and an intention to do what they believe to be God's will. The sincerity of this attitude of faith is shown in the fidelity to what is known of that divine will, and finally to the natural law written in their hearts: "When Gentiles who have not the law do by nature what the law requires, they are a law to

---

which in fact truly may be God. For, as a result of our spiritual weakness, there can easily be a discordance between what in reality we believe and the ideas in which we express to ourselves what we believe." St Thomas' analysis of man's basic moral choice (Ia–IIae, q. 89, a. 6) is a help towards understanding this problem which I can do no more than mention here.

themselves, even though they do not have the law. They show that what the law requires is written on their hearts, while their conscience also bears witness and their conflicting thoughts accuse or perhaps excuse them...." (Rom 2 : 14–15.)

This then is the religious situation of the non-evangelised, whether because they lived before Christ, or because they were prevented from being evangelised by obstacles not of their own making. It is not, as we have seen, a desperate situation, but it is precarious and obviously less favourable to salvation than an explicit faith in Christ and visible membership in the church; for within the church man finds not only greater security, but the fullness of the light of revelation, the riches of sacramental life, the support of the ecclesial community, the help of the hierarchy in his life of faith, in his search for goodness and in putting his charity into practice. And if the non-evangelised *are* saved, their salvation is not outside Christ or apart from the church: it is Christ's grace that saves them and acts upon them, and it is towards the mystery of Christ that they are tending without realising it, by their general disposition to do God's will, and thus to enter the plan of salvation as designed by God.

The salvation of the Jews

Before Christ's coming

The problem of the salvation of Jews as presented earlier belongs to the New Testament, but it is important to recall what the Jews' situation was in regard to salvation under the old covenant. The election of Israel did nothing to worsen the situation of the Gentiles, but it placed the Jews in a more favourable situation in regard to salvation because of revelation, the law and the religious institutions God gave his people. While continuing to manifest himself to all through his works, God revealed himself to the Jews in a more definite, and ever more precise manner. The Israelites' response to that revelation was belief in Yahweh—and this was a more explicit and more enlightened faith than the faith of the Gentiles. It was expressed in a religion chosen by God himself when he gave his people their institutions of worship. And it was carried over into life by the fulfilment of the law received on Sinai. This was the framework in which the salvation of the Jews took place under the old covenant, and it was the norm for them until such time as Christ should come to fulfil the law in the gospel.

However, the Israelite religious structure was not *of itself* the source of salvation: when an Israelite was saved it was in reference to Christ and through Christ. His faith was directed towards Christ, for he believed in the God whose promise was to be fulfilled in Jesus, and who chose Israel as his own people in view of the Saviour to come; the scriptures in which he found the word of the Lord were underlined with messianic hopes; the forms of worship whereby he lived his faith were directed towards the perfect and final sacrifice of Christ, and even the law was simply a custodian leading to him. (Gal 3 : 24.) Furthermore, the grace whereby the Israelite was justified and given the strength to fulfil the prescriptions of the law faithfully was given to him only in view of the merits of the Christ who was to come.

Since Christ's coming

"He came to his own home, and his own people received him not." (Jn 1 : 11.) Israel, the chosen people, did not receive Christ, did not enter the church, and as a people they find themselves outside the way of salvation. In point of fact, the incredulity of Israel does not pose any particularly difficult problem to theological thinking if looked at on the individual level. For, in effect, the Jew who culpably rejects belief in the gospel places himself in the same situation as anyone to whom it has been announced and who knowingly rejects it; and on the other hand, if the non-evangelised can be saved with only an implicit faith in Christ, then *a fortiori* the Jew who believes himself bound in conscience to follow his religion can be saved with a faith that is actually directed towards Christ—whom he fails to recognise through no fault of his own. Though, since the gospel has been promulgated, that religion is no longer the normal way to God, it is better than the way of the pagan who has no positive revelation at all; and the faith of the Israelite is more explicitly directed towards Christ as the hope of Israel than the faith of the pagan can possibly be.

No, the incredulity of Israel only becomes a difficulty when one comes to examine the historic role of the chosen people in God's plan. This is the point of view from which St Paul writes chapters 9–11 of Romans, and one must remember that fact if one is not to pose the wrong problems when reading them. In them we find the echo of the discussions Paul must have had on the subject with his Jewish and Judeo-Christian friends. Examining by turns the points of view of God and of Israel, he begins by showing that the incredulity of the chosen people, which is culpable (Rom 10 : 14–21), does not compromise the fidelity of God, nor provide any justification for accusing God of injustice. Then, raising his eyes to a total view of the divine plan, Paul declares that God has not rejected his people, and that following the same law that governed God's action in the Old Testament, there is still today a faithful remnant in Israel who have come to the gospel: "I ask, then, has God rejected his people? By no means! I myself am an Israelite, a descendant of Abraham, a member of the tribe of Benjamin. God has not rejected his people whom he foreknew. Do you not know what the scripture says of Elijah, how he pleads with God . . . [and God replies] I have kept for myself seven thousand men who have not bowed the knee to Baal. So too at the present time there is a remnant, chosen by grace." (Rom 11 : 1–5.)

Furthermore, the incredulity of Israel was permitted in order that the Gentiles might more easily come to the gospel. "Through their trespass salvation has come to the Gentiles... their failure means riches for the Gentiles." (Rom 11 : 11–12.)

The very first persecution, in fact, made it impossible for the early community to turn in upon themselves, and so precipitated the proclamation of the gospel outside Jerusalem and Palestine (Ac 8 : 1–4; 11 : 19–21; and *passim*); it was the rejection by the Jews that led St Paul to announce the word to the Gentiles in the cities where he preached (Ac 13 : 46; 18 : 6–7; 19 : 9); it was the presence of so many converts from paganism in the primitive church that led to such a rapid abandonment of the now outworn Jewish prescriptions; and lastly, from the psychological point of view, if the Jews had entered the church in a body they might have proved an obstacle to the conversion of many Gentiles who would have been likely to think of Christianity as simply a Jewish sect belonging exclusively to Palestine.

Israel's incredulity is not final. St Paul solemnly declares that Israel will be converted to the great spiritual benefit of all when the whole of the pagan world enters the church: "Lest you be wise in your own conceits, I want you to understand this mystery, brethren: a hardening has come upon part of Israel, until the full number of the Gentiles come in, and so all Israel will be saved.... For if their rejection means the reconciliation of the world, what will their acceptance mean but life from the dead." (Rom 11 : 25–6, 15.)

What exactly does Paul mean by saying that all the Gentiles will enter the church, or all Israel will be saved? How and when will these religious events come about? It is impossible to answer such questions exactly. "To interpret all this teaching in modern terms, imagine that St Paul is projecting against a backcloth ... all the history that was to follow Christ's coming. The conversion of Israel is not thus necessarily a total volte-face that will take place immediately before the Parousia. The prophecy may well be fulfilled by successive returns to the Christian Church, which will always be the spiritual Israel. Nor need we base our thinking too much on the concrete quantities suggested by the notions of mass, fullness or totality. St Paul does not treat such questions of number in the same way as we would. God will save all Israel in principle. It is for him to decide how many will visibly join the church over the years."[1]

Seeing the divine plan, by which the infidelity of Israel, after having enabled the Gentiles to enter the church, culminates in a conversion that will also be of inestimable supernatural benefit to them, arouses in St Paul a sense of contemplative admiration for God's merciful wisdom: "O the depth of the riches and wisdom and knowledge of God! How unsearchable are his judge-

[1] L. Cerfaux, *Une lecture de l'épître aux Romains*, Paris 1947, 105.

ments and how inscrutable his ways! For who has known the mind of the Lord, or who has been his counsellor? Or who has given a gift to him that he might be repaid? For from him and through him and to him are all things. To him be glory forever. Amen. (Rom 11 : 33–6.)

Christian attitudes

Towards the Jews

Before dealing with the problem of Israel's incredulity, St Paul enumerates with delight the religious privileges of the chosen people of whose race "according to the flesh, is the Christ" (Rom 9: 4–5), and, having indicated that their incredulity has been permitted for the sake of the Gentiles' conversion, he urges humility on Christians who have come from paganism: "If some of the branches were broken off, and you, a wild olive shoot, were grafted in their place to share the richness of the olive tree, do not boast over the branches." (11 : 17–18.)

The attitude of Christians towards the Jews who have not embraced Christianity should have no room for scorn: we respect in them those whose ancestors were the people of the promise, and we are too well aware of God's grace in bringing us to Christ to feel any pride when we see those who have not yet found him. Knowing that all men have been redeemed by Christ, and that all are called to salvation, we must take care not to deceive ourselves by translating into religious terms a racialist feeling we dare not admit to, and we must treat *all* men, "Jews and Greeks", with the same fraternal charity. Knowing God's plan for Israel, we sincerely long for their entry into the church, and must do what we can to prepare for it: "Brethren, my heart's desire and prayer to God for them is that they may be saved." (Rom 10 : 1.)

Towards the non-evangelised

Christians must take care not to have a closed mind towards pagans, for we know that Christ died for all men, that his grace acts beyond the bounds of the circle of the baptised,[1] and that those who do not visibly belong to the church can be disposed towards the mystical body of the Redeemer "by some unconscious yearning and desire".[2] We must abstain from falsely conceived apologetics which lead us to depreciate the real values of non-Christian religions in order to show the splendour of Christianity.[3]

But this openness of mind does not lead us to any kind of indifferentism in religion. We believe that the truth given by Christ is something for which there is no substitute, that it can be found nowhere outside revelation, and is in-

[1] Pope Alexander VIII condemned the proposition: "that pagans, Jews, heretics and others like them never in any way receive the slightest influence from Jesus Christ". See *Lumière et Vie*, 18, 49.

[2] Encyclical *Mystici Corporis Christi*, London 1946, §102, 61.

[3] J. Daniélou, *The Lord of History*, 108.

tended for all men. Nothing must make us forget that, except in exceptional circumstances, since the gospel has been promulgated it is necessary for salvation to belong to Christ and the church by faith and baptism, and that knowing God's mind upon the church and refusing to join it is to refuse salvation. We know that, even for the non-evangelised, all other ways remain imperfect and precarious, and we make our own the Pope's invitation "to yield their free consent to the inner stirrings of God's grace and strive to extricate themselves from a state in which they cannot be secure of their own eternal salvation; for though they may be related to the Mystical Body of the Redeemer by some unconscious yearning and desire, yet they are deprived of those many and great heavenly gifts and aids which can be enjoyed only in the Catholic Church".[1]

Belonging to that church which is willed by its Head to be essentially missionary, and knowing that men can only find in communion with her the full conditions for salvation, the Christian who sees the de-Christianisation of some countries, and the fact that so many of his fellow men are pagans, becomes more vitally aware of his missionary duty, and of the impossibility of living a Christian life without an apostolic dimension. Faced with a world that does not know Christ, he sees more clearly the part he

[1] *Mystici Corporis*, 61.

must take in making the church more present and announcing the gospel.

Reading

Wis 13: 1–9; Ac 14: 15–17; 17: 22–8; Rom 1: 18–21; 2: 12–16; 9: 1 – 11: 36; Heb 11

14

The return of Christ

Faith in Christ's return

From the very beginning, the faith of Christians has been oriented towards Christ's second coming; with his own words as the basis, this is reaffirmed throughout the New Testament, from the account of the ascension to the Book of Revelation. During his ministry, Jesus spoke several times of his return (Lk 18 : 8), and especially in his eschatological discourse: "In those days ... the sun will be darkened, and the moon will not give its light, and the stars will be falling from heaven, and the powers in the heavens will be shaken. And then they will see the Son of man coming in clouds with great power and glory. And he will send out the angels, and gather his elect from the four winds, from the ends of the earth to the ends of heaven." (Mk 13 : 24–7.)

The announcement made to the apostles after the ascension refers to the same event: "Men of Galilee, why do you stand looking into heaven? This Jesus who was taken up from you into heaven, will come in the same way as you saw him go into heaven." (Ac 1 : 11.)

The thought of the Lord's return constantly recurs in the letters of St Paul, and the author of Hebrews was only expressing the belief of all when he wrote: "Christ, having been offered once to bear the sins of many, will appear a second time, not to deal with sin but to save those who are eagerly waiting for him." (11 : 28.)

The Book of Revelation itself, sustained throughout by hope in Christ's return, concludes with the wish used in the liturgy of the early Christian communities, "Come, Lord Jesus!" (22 : 20.)

Faith in Christ's return, and hope for his coming have never ceased to inspire the church, and one could fill books with texts from the Fathers on the subject of the Lord's coming in glory at the end of time. It is enough to quote the passage of the Creed which expressed the faith of Christians from the very first in "Jesus Christ, the only Son of God . . . who will return in glory to judge the living and the dead".

There are a great many unanswered questions on the subject of Christ's return. When will it be? How will the events of the end of the world unfold? What will become of the present world? What difference will the Lord's second coming make to the mystery of salvation? Of them all, this last is by far the most fundamental. Unfortunately it sometimes happens that questions unimportant by comparison—such as the date of the Parousia, or how it will come about—get all the attention to the detriment of that one. Revelation, as we shall see, does little to encourage curiosity; on the other hand it does give answers to the questions that are of direct importance to the believer.

Vocabulary and literary form

Before examining those answers, we must be clear about the exact meaning of certain terms to do with the end of the world, and say something of the descriptions given of it in the New Testament.

To designate the doctrine that deals with the end of present realities—man, the world—we use the term *eschatology*, a word made up of the Greek *eschatos*, last, and *logos*, teaching. Thus we speak of the eschatology of the prophets, meaning their prophecies about the Messiah and the end of time which he was to inaugurate; of the eschatological character of Christian life, because it is eternal life already begun; or simply of eschatology, meaning the return of Christ, the general resurrection, the judgement and the world to come.

Another Greek word is used for the glorious coming of Christ at the end of time: the word *parousia*, which means presence, coming, arrival. In Corinthians, for instance, St Paul speaks of those who belong to Christ "at his coming (parousia)". (1 Cor 15:23.) In the same epistle, he also uses the term "the Day of our Lord Jesus Christ": in this case it is a phrase borrowed from the Old Testament, where the "Day of Yahweh" means the day of God's intervention and judgement (Am 5 : 18; Jl 1 : 15; 2 : 1–2), now used to mean the return of Christ, the sovereign Judge, at the end of the world. That is why St Paul exhorts the Corinthians to behave in such a way as to be "guiltless in the day of our Lord Jesus Christ". (1 Cor 1 : 8.)

We also find in St Paul the Jewish distinction between the present age, or this age, and the future age, or the age to come. "The present age" is the present time considered in its pejorative aspect, in its connection with original sin which dominates it by subjecting the history that fills it to the power of evil. "The future age", on the other hand, is the time to come which is characterised by God's victory over the powers of evil, and by the peace and joy that accompany it.[1] Unlike the Jewish conception of two successive ages, the Pauline picture includes a time between the coming of Christ and his return when the two ages interpenetrate: we still live in the present age, but victory is already won in Christ who unceasingly sanctifies the world by his Holy Spirit. However, the effects of that victory will only be fully felt in the world to come.[2]

We return to Greek etymology with the word *apocalypse*: it means "revelation", and has become a kind of title for the work written by

---

[1] See Oscar Cullmann, *Christ and Time*, London 1962 (revised edition), 47.

[2] We find this distinction made, for instance in 1 Cor 2 : 6, where Paul speaks of the "wisdom of this age", and the "rulers of this age".

John on Patmos. (Rev 1 : 9–10.) Yet we must not forget that there are in the bible and other Jewish writings, especially those from around the Christian era, quite a number of apocalypses (Ezek 39–38; Dn 7–12; Zech 9–14; Ez 4) and that they belong to a definite literary genre. Their authors' object is to hand on a revelation about the future, and to do so they use symbols and images to translate the message they have received which must not be taken too literally, but valued as symbols. This must be remembered when we read the visions of the Book of Revelation.

In a more general way, too, it is interesting to note from what sources Christ or the authors of the New Testament take some of the images in the descriptions they give of eschatological events: this may help us to assess the exact value of those descriptions, and their importance as doctrine. To herald the most important of all theophanies—that of the end of time—the New-Testament writers once more make use of some of the detail from the Old-Testament theophanies. St Paul writes that, at the moment of Christ's second coming, "We shall all be changed, in a moment, in the twinkling of an eye, at the last trumpet. For the trumpet will sound, and the dead will be raised imperishable." (1 Cor 15 : 51–2.)

"That trumpet is part of the traditional apocalyptic arsenal of Judaism; it brings into eschatology an element belonging properly to the description of God's descent upon Sinai"[1]; for, if you recall, the exodus account mentioned a loud trumpet sound, which was in fact the violent noise of the wind accompanying Yahweh's manifesting himself. (Ex 19 : 16–19.) In St Paul's description, that trumpet is obviously only an image, but an image with a meaning: it indicates that the resurrection will take place at a moment willed by God, and will be a shattering manifestation of his power.

The New-Testament writers and Jesus himself, take up certain images from the apocalyptic passages of the prophets; these make use of certain stereotyped images in describing the cosmic cataclysms that accompany the major interventions of divine power: the sun grows dark, the moon turns into blood, the stars fall from the sky, the earth quakes, the heavens tremble. (Is 13 : 9–10; Ezek 32 : 7–8; Jl 2 : 10–11; 3 : 1–5.) Even without considering whether the totality of these images really indicate some kind of cosmic upheaval, it is clear that their stereotyped character shows that they should not be interpreted strictly as to detail.

The parousia

The parousia is an event so rich and complex that it cannot be defined in a few words, but must be described bit by bit in its different aspects. It is, in essence, the glorious and final

[1] Dom Jacques Dupont, OSB, *L'union avec le Christ suivant saint Paul*, Louvain 1952, 68–9.

coming of the Lord Jesus at the end of time, his return awaited in faith by the church ever since the ascension. This event will be of capital importance to all mankind and even to the cosmos itself.

The parousia will mark the end of this world and the advent of a new world. In the gospel Jesus boldly declares: "Heaven and earth will pass away, but my words will not pass away." (Mk 13 : 31.)

And the visionary of Revelation writes: "I saw a new heaven and a new earth; for the first heaven and the first earth had passed away, and the sea was no more." (21 : 1.)

One could go on listing texts proclaiming the end of the world, but what matters more is to consider what is their precise meaning; have they a purely symbolic sense, meant to stress the magnificence of God's intervention when the Lord returns, or have they a more literal sense implying a transformation of the created universe? In general, the traditional interpretation has not been content with a purely symbolic exegesis, but given them a more literal sense. It seems then, that under some aspect and in some way, the present world will come to an end one day to give place to another world. But, having stated this in principle, it is not possible to specify exactly the manner or nature of the change. The author of 2 Peter presents it as a total break between the present world and the new one, with the first disappearing "in a kind of catastrophic incineration", as M.-E. Boismard, OP, puts it[1]: "The day of the Lord will come like a thief, and then the heavens will pass away with a loud noise, and the elements will be dissolved with fire, and the earth and the works that are upon it will be burnt up." (2 Pt 3 : 10.)

But here again one may wonder how much is symbol and how much reality, given that Jewish tradition saw purifying fire as an instrument of God's judgement, and that the theme of the destruction of the world by fire was at that time widespread in Greco-Roman philosophy.[2]

The Pauline presentation is quite different, showing the world to come as nothing other than the present world wonderfully transformed and renewed at the touch of the divine glory. For St Paul "the return of Christ takes place in the perspective of this world, not in some 'heaven' of indeterminate locality",[3] and creation does not vanish to give place to another world, but is purified, freed from its enslavement to vanity. It would seem then that Paul, who is in any case cautious on the subject of the new heavens and new earth, "did not foresee that the universe would be destroyed and created afresh".[4] For St Paul this entire conception is tied in with the theme of Christ as the new Adam whose head-

[1] M.-E. Boismard, OP, "Le retour du Christ", in *Lumière et Vie*, 11, 63.
[2] Boismard, in "Le retour du Christ", and in the Jerusalem Bible on this epistle.
[3] Boismard, "Le retour du Christ", 64.
[4] J. Bonsirven, *L'évangile de Paul*, Paris 1948, 332.

ship extends to the whole universe, and not to mankind alone. The return of the Lord will have cosmic repercussions, and will mark a "renewal" for the world under the effects of God's glory.

The parousia is principally the time of the resurrection of all, either for life or for damnation: "The hour is coming when all who are in the tombs will hear his voice and come forth, those who have done good, to the resurrection of life, and those who have done evil, to the resurrection of judgement." (Jn 5 : 28–9.) It will be, in effect, the judgement of all men by Christ: "When the Son of man comes in his glory, and all the angels with him, then he will sit on his glorious throne. Before him will be gathered all the nations, and he will separate them one from another as a shepherd separates the sheep from the goats." (Mt 25 : 31–2.) In speaking of the last judgement, Jesus insists on the importance of brotherly love: "Come, O blessed of my Father ... for I was hungry and you gave me food, I was thirsty and you gave me drink, I was a stranger and you welcomed me. ... Depart from me, you cursed, into the eternal fire prepared for the devil and his angels; for I was hungry and you gave me no food, I was thirsty and you gave me no drink, I was a stranger and you did not welcome me. ..." (Mt 25 : 34–5, 41–3.)

St Paul reminds Timothy of the importance of faith in relation to the judgement: " I charge you in the presence of God and of Christ Jesus who is to judge the living and the dead, and by his appearing and his kingdom: preach the word. ... For I am already on the point of being sacrificed; the time of my departure has come. I have fought the good fight, I have finished the race, I have kept the faith. Henceforth there is laid up for me the crown of righteousness, which the Lord, the righteous judge, will award to me on that day, and not only to me but also to all who have loved his appearing." (2 Tim 4 : 1–2, 6–8.)

Faith, hope and charity: these are the virtues that sum up and contain all the others, the virtues the Christian must live, in expectation of the Lord, if he is to be with him in the kingdom.

After the judgement, Christ will give back the kingdom to his Father: "In Christ shall all be made alive. But each in his own order: Christ the first fruits; then, at his coming, those who belong to Christ. Then comes the end, when he delivers the kingdom to God the Father after destroying every rule and every authority and every power." (1 Cor 15 : 22–4.)

Then the plan of salvation will be complete.

The completion of the history of salvation

The parousia, which is on the horizon of this age, will in fact mark the completion of the history of salvation. It will be its *completion*—not merely its final point or its conclusion, but the final and perfect consecration of that history: "We shall always be with the Lord." (1 Thes 4 : 17.)

It is the completion of *the history of salvation*. In the third chapter of Genesis, the biblical writer used symbols to describe the first sin and its consequences: the break between man and God, figured by his expulsion from the Garden of Eden, his tendency towards evil, death, suffering, and the discord between man and the rest of material creation: "Thorns and thistles the ground shall bring forth to you; and you shall eat the plants of the field." (Gn 3 : 18.)

At the parousia, the elect will be forever set apart from the domain of sin; they will receive in its fullness the friendship of God who will be "everything to everyone", and will establish his dwelling among men (Rev 21 : 3); the resurrection of their bodies, become incorruptible by the life-giving action of the Holy Spirit, will mark "the total realisation of their condition as spiritual men"[1] and the universal triumph of Christ over death: "The last enemy to be destroyed is death." (1 Cor 15 : 26.)

Suffering will disappear. "God will wipe away every tear from their eyes, and death shall be no more, neither shall there be mourning nor crying nor pain any more, for the former things have passed away." (Rev 21 : 4.)

The material creation will be freed from the slavery of vanity: "The creation waits with eager

---

[1] J. Schmitt, *Jésus ressuscité dans la prédication apostolique*, Paris 1949, 47. Note that the word "spiritual" is not synonymous with "immaterial", but indicates the quality of whatever is under the influence of the Holy Spirit.

longing for the revealing of the sons of God; for the creation was subject to futility, not of its own will but by the will of him who subjected it in hope; because the creation itself will be set free from its bondage to decay and obtain the glorious liberty of the children of God. We know that the whole creation has been groaning in travail together until now." (Rom 8 : 19–22.)

In associating the material world with the glory of the children of God, one must specially remember the fact that, through the intermediary of risen man, creation will once more be in contact with God's glory, and return to its normal place in relation to God, for it will be totally brought back to God by man whom he originally placed in dominion over it. (Gn 1 : 28.) The Lord's return will thus mark the completion of his victory over sin and the goal of the mystery of redemption.

The parousia is the completion of salvation both for the individual and for the community. Those who have slept in the Lord will know him face to face in the vision which takes the place of faith and hope, and in the charity that remains. (1 Cor 13 : 8–13.) At the moment of the Lord's return, the resurrection, which will bring each one personally to the fullness of salvation, will at the same time be the completion for the community of the history of salvation. The resurrection, the final state of development of the body of Christ, will be the triumph of Christ and of all his church. In God's plan, the members of the people of God will only be fully saved at the moment when the people as a whole is saved.

This completion of the history of salvation will take place in Christ, will happen at the moment of his return: the elect will be forever with the Lord, saved by the fullness of his grace. In Jesus, the new Adam, the divine plan to "unite all things in him, things in heaven and things on earth" will be fulfilled. And finally, it is he who, having completed his saving mission, will hand back the kingdom to his Father; "the People God has won, for the praise of his glory". (Eph 1 : 10, 14.)[1]

When the parousia will be

The church's hopes are wholly turned towards the return of the Lord, and it is only natural for Christians to have wondered when it would happen, and to have looked for an answer in scripture. But in fact what scripture has to tell is little enough; there is only really one very clear statement about the day and the hour of the parousia, and merely an indication of some of the events which must happen before the end of time.

That the date of Christ's return is a secret which God keeps for himself, and which it is not for man to know, Jesus solemnly proclaimed in his eschatological discourse: "Of that day or that hour no one knows, not even the angels in heaven, nor the Son, but only the Father." (Mk

[1] Following the Jerusalem Bible translation.

13 : 32.) A statement as clear as this should be enough to discourage any Christian from wasting time on useless speculations about the date, and to make him put into practice our Lord's advice: "Watch therefore—for you do not know when the master of the house will come." (Mk 13 : 35.)

But God has revealed certain events which will take place before the parousia. As we saw in the previous chapter, the conversion of Israel as a people will happen between now and the end of the world, once the whole pagan world has had access to the church. This statement apart, we can draw no precise conclusion about the date of the parousia: for, first of all, we do not know whether the conversion of Israel will happen suddenly, or come about over a long period; and secondly, we cannot say with certainty whether the parousia will come immediately afterwards or not. St Paul's text on the subject can be interpreted in various ways: "If their rejection means the reconciliation of the world, what will their acceptance mean but life from the dead?" (Rom 11 : 15.)

To a number of exegetes, this means the final resurrection, which will follow the conversion of the Jews after a longer or shorter interval; but some, translating literally "a life from among the dead" think that the apostle means only to indicate that the conversion of Israel will be of extraordinary supernatural benefit to the church, and therefore they see no connection of any kind in time between the conversion of Israel and the parousia. All they take it to mean is that Israel will be converted before the end of the world.

The important text of 2 Thessalonians (2 : 1–12), and some passages from Revelation (12; 20 : 7–10), are normally taken to mean[1] that, "before the coming of the last times, the church must undergo a generalised and tremendous assault from the pagan nations, an assault that will imperil her very existence".[2] But neither this, nor the preceding information, makes it possible to determine the precise moment of the parousia; for the persecutions directed against the church are in a sense part of her pilgrim condition, and the normal tendency of the persecuted is to identify the trial of the moment with the great persecution of the end of time; and further, it is hard to interpret the details of the description of the great assault against the church: exegetes are far from agreed as to the identity of the "adversary" spoken of by St Paul

[1] That the final phase of the struggle is, thanks to the power of Satan and his false prodigies, to be the most violent and dangerous, has even "been contested, for the gospel says nothing of the kind, which leads one to wonder whether either in St Paul, or in Revelation, we must not allow something for a literary style that dramatises the final episode of the fight with a recrudescence of persecution and unleashing of evil, in order to cast an even brighter light on the blazing, irresistible and sudden nature of Christ's triumph." (An opinion quoted by F. Amiot, *Epîtres aux Thessaloniciens*, Paris 1946, 274, n. 3.) Though this opinion does not represent the exegesis generally accepted today, it is worth knowing that it exists.

[2] Boismard, "Le retour du Christ", 69–70.

—whether it means an individual or a collective one—and the nature of "him who restrains it". (2 Thes 2 : 7.)[1] We must, then, remember the sign that has been foretold, but as for the date of the parousia, all we can do is hold on to the Lord's word: "Take heed, watch; for you do not know when the time will come." (Mk 13 : 33.)

The Christian in expectation of the parousia

Though Christians are not called upon to know the date of the parousia, their whole attitude is none the less governed by the certainty that it will take place. Moving with the church towards the kingdom, they live in hope of the Lord's return, and this gives all that they do now an eschatological dimension.

We make ours the prayer of the first Christians, "Come Lord Jesus." (Rev 22 : 20.) And when we take part in the celebration of the eucharist, we remember Paul's words: "As often as you eat this bread and drink the cup, you proclaim the Lord's death until he comes." (1 Cor 11 : 26.)

The certainty that Christ will return fills us with joy, a joy all the deeper in that we have received Christ's grace and the "first fruits of the Spirit" (Rom 8 : 23) in baptism. Difficulties, persecution and suffering do not lead to discouragement, for they are the cross we are called

[1] For a detailed study of these texts, some such commentary on them as B. Rigaux, OFM, *Les épîtres aux Thessaloniciens*, Paris 1956.

upon as Christ's disciples to bear (Mk 8 : 34), and the path leading to the resurrection: "I consider that the sufferings of this present time are not worth comparing with the glory that is to be revealed to us." (Rom 8 : 18.)

Ours is no naïve and unthinking joy, nor must we forget the invitation to vigilance contained in the gospel: if Christ's love is the moving power of our lives, we are aware of our own weakness. To be a Christian means prayer, self-sacrifice, and a clear-sighted fidelity to Christ's love— never rejecting it and so placing oneself outside the plan of redemption: "I pommel my body and subdue it, lest after preaching to others I myself should be disqualified." (1 Cor 9:27.) The thought of the Lord's return makes Christians place the essence of their hope in the Kingdom: "What does it profit a man to gain the whole world and forfeit his life?" (Mk 8 : 36.)

It leads us to bring a certain wisdom to bear on things and events in view of the unfolding of history, and to live with detachment in this world whose figure passes. (1 Cor 7:31.) For whether he lives a celibate life, the better to serve God and his brethren, or whether he practises poverty and self-giving in all the situations and commitments involved in the lay state, the Christian, by his detachment, bears witness to the value-judgements of the gospel. That same judgement leads him to attach the greatest importance to the proclamation of Christ's message, to which all men are called to belong at the moment of the parousia.

The expectation of the Lord's return, which enables the Christian to estimate all things at their true value, does not develop in him to any kind of scorn for mankind and the created world, nor to indifference to the human community in which charity demands that he take his proper place. St Paul's forceful statements in 2 Thessalonians leave us in no doubt about this. The Christian's attitude is eschatological, but "it is the eschatology of St Paul and not that of the *illuminati* of Thessalonica, and it certainly does not imply (as some people appear to think) neglect of the duties of the present, lack of interest in this existence, or a putting of charity into cold storage until the end of the world."[1]

Reading

Mk 8:1–37; Mt 25:31–46; 1 Cor 7:29–31; 15:22–8; 1 Thes 4:13 – 5:11; 2 Thes 2:3; Rev 21:22

[1] H. de Lubac, *The Splendour of the Church*, London 1956, 190.

15

The bible, light of our life

I began this book by asking whether the bible contains a *mystique*—that is to say, a vision of the world and of history which moves man to act, and directs his action. Each stage of God's plan has in turn provided the elements for an affirmative answer: we have noted the universal dimension of each, its place in the history of the world's salvation, its repercussions on life. In this way we have, bit by bit, brought out the original vision of the world and of history that God reveals in the bible, and which inspires Christians to act, and determines how they shall do so. By this very fact, the bible appears as a light for living by, and it is in this guise that it is best to conclude our picture of the mystery of salvation as a whole, repeating perhaps a few of the things we have already discovered.

Revelation of God as directing the history of salvation

The bible is the light of our life for several reasons. First, because it makes known the God who directs the history of salvation. From the creation to the parousia, it is one and the same God who is carrying out his plan in the world: the Creator, the God of Abraham, Isaac and Jacob, the God who spoke through the prophets, the God who has revealed himself as Father, Son and Holy Spirit, is the one God, the principle and end of all that exists: "There is one God, the Father, from whom are all things and for whom we exist, and one Lord, Jesus Christ, through whom are all things and through whom we exist." (1 Cor 8 : 6.)

He is a God who makes himself known. He makes himself known through his works: "The heavens are telling the glory of God; and the firmament proclaims his handiwork." (Ps 19 : 1.) And he makes himself known in the words he speaks to mankind, in his behaviour towards his people, and supremely, in the incarnation: the bible is the light of life because it contains the revelation of him who is the Light and the Life. (Jn 8 : 18.)

The God of the bible is also the transcendent God, Lord of history, being both its guide and its goal, and giving it its meaning by entering it himself. He is the God of love, "merciful and gracious" (Ex 34 : 6),[1] and is similar to the almost physical love of a mother who cannot help having mercy on the child she has given birth to, however he has sinned. God's love is pictured by

[1] The root *raham*, which serves to translate the merciful tenderness of God, suggests the emotion of a mother's love.

the prophets in the guise of the loftiest of all human loves, that of a man for his wife, and a mother for her child. The history of salvation is made up of all the things God has done for men: the creation, the covenant, the redemptive incarnation, the founding of the church, the giving of the Holy Spirit. And God manifests his transcendence in this very love whose ways are so baffling to human understanding: the folly of the cross, which is the wisdom of God (1 Cor 1 : 18, 23–4; 2 : 19), the beatitudes which are such a contradiction of the world's conception of happiness, and so on. "For my thoughts are not your thoughts, neither are your ways my ways, says the Lord. For as the heavens are higher than the earth, so are my ways higher than your ways, and my thoughts than your thoughts." (Is 55 : 8–9.)

God of the promises and of the covenant, the Lord is, finally, the faithful God, who never fails, upon whom one can always depend: "God is faithful, by whom you were called into the fellowship of his Son, Jesus Christ our Lord." (1 Cor 1 : 9.)

A mystique of worldwide dimensions

The bible is also our light because the mystique it contains is universal. Bible history goes from Genesis to the Book of Revelation: it begins with the creation of the world, and concludes in the "new heavens and new earth". The parousia will mark the primacy of Christ, the

Saviour, over all creation, which "waits with eager longing for the revealing of the sons of God" (Rom 8 : 19), and the drawing together of all things in Christ to fulfil God's eternal plan. (Eph 1 : 10.) The call to salvation is a universal one, for Christ died for all, and God wills all men to be saved. The church is universal, with its mission to preach the gospel to the whole world, and to bring together in Christ all men and all human values. Everyone who responds to the divine call will be totally saved, body and soul; here Christianity differs from the Greek idea of salvation meaning being set free from matter. To us, creation came from God's hands good, and salvation means purifying it from sin: Christians are neither materialist nor falsely spiritualist, but optimistic and clearsighted in their view of the world.

Showing the meaning of world history

The bible mystique, cosmic in scope, also makes clear the meaning of history. It no more dispenses the historian from investigating events and civilisations, than the knowledge of creation dispenses the scientist from studying geology, but it gives a revealed vision of the moving force of history which is of capital importance.

In the bible, history is not a constant renewing of things—even though similar events may recur because men are all alike, and because they are inclined to sin: the meaning of history is linear, not cyclic. It is a series of once-for-all events moving towards the same goal (the creation, the election of Abraham, the covenant, the incarnation, Christ's passover, the founding of the church, Pentecost...), and is made up of individual personal lives, real and irreplaceable.

The purpose of bible history is to set man free in Christ, who has brought him the Truth and the Life, and his freedom will be complete at the parousia. "The movement of history, as the Marxists say, and we agree with them, is to set man free, but we say that Christ alone can do it, Christ and those who prolong his existence ... What constitutes the special content of Christianity and makes it unquestionably transcendent, is Jesus Christ, the Son of God, who gives us salvation."[1]

The bible therefore enables the believer to see the profound meaning of history; for in fact there are not two more or less parallel histories going on in the world—human history composed of the succession of empires, and another history more or less artificially hooked on to it. There is only one history, whose more immediately eventful aspect is described in the history books, and whose deepest and richest reality is affirmed by those who have faith in God's word. While events develop and civilisations follow one another, the history of the body of Christ is also taking place, as it continues growing until the Lord's return: "In the eyes of a Christian, the historical appearances are no more than the shadows of real history, the history that is now

[1] J. Daniélou, *The Lord of History*, 80 and 118.

written down, which neither historians nor even hagiographers can put into words, and which, while happening in time, is imprinted upon eternity and will be recapitulated on the last day by Christ the Judge. This is Sacred History, the only true history, profound, secret, as inward as the glory of the King's daughter; it is the history of mankind, created, fallen and saved, going towards its consummation, which is God's return in all-embracing love, by the progressive completion of the mystical body. In this sense the church is making history, and is alone in making it, with profane events figuring only as its phenomena and conditions. Just as the church moves towards identification with the human race, so the church's history is moving towards identification with the history of mankind which has become sacred history."[1]

Casting light on the present situation of Christians

Christians, engaged as they are in sacred history, and living already in Christ, find themselves on earth in a religious situation which has not yet reached completion, and which may seem paradoxical for several reasons. The bible explains several aspects of it.

The Christian is not "of the world" though living in the world: because he is regenerated by the grace of baptism, he is not of the world

[1] J. Folliet, "L'Eglise dans l'histoire", in *Informations Catholiques internationales*, 1 Feb. 1956, 3.

which rejects the light of God and fights against Christ, and yet he lives in the world. (Jn 17 : 11, 15–16.) He collaborates in extending the kingdom of God, working unceasingly to make the city of this world one of brotherhood. The central object of his hopes is the return of the Lord and the development of the body of Christ to its full stature, but his work for human brotherhood is an effect and sign of the charity in which he must make ready for Christ's second coming and labour for the building up of Christ's body (Eph 4 : 16): "If any one has the world's goods and sees his brother in need, and closes his heart against him, how does God's love abide in him?" (1 Jn 3 : 17.)

Furthermore, he does not live his Christianity as an isolated individual, but as a person belonging to a people: personally justified at the moment of baptism, every Christian is known and loved Christ "by name" (Jn 10 : 3, 14), and will be judged according to his own personal responsibilities, but his salvation takes place within the church, in the unity of the body of Christ, and it will be finally achieved only at the general resurrection when it is achieved for the whole people of God.

In the present situation, salvation is already won for the Christian, but it could still be lost; though Christians are cleansed from sin by baptism, they have not been made impeccable. Living a new life in Christ and possessing the first fruits of the Spirit, they are already saved in essence; yet baptism gives no automatic assurance of salvation, and they must follow our Lord's advice to watch always, being faithful to the gospel and avoiding anything which will place them outside the way established by the Lord. For, fundamentally, salvation is a gift to which man must respond freely.

No one lays more stress on its being a gift than St Paul: "God, who is rich in mercy, out of the great love with which he loved us, even when we were dead through our trespasses, made us alive together with Christ. By grace you have been saved." (Eph 2 : 4–5.) But God has created man in his own image, intelligent and free, and does not force salvation upon him; worked upon by grace, man accepts it freely in faith and spends his life responding to it. Here again, St Paul is absolutely clear, as a glance through his epistles will show. So the Christian's attitude is at once that of the poor man who receives everything from God and lives in faith, humility and trust, that of the prophet who declares and repeats the message of salvation with power given him by God, and that of the sage who, enlightened by God, applies the revelation he has been given to his daily life.

Christian spirituality takes its inspiration from three events in Christ's mystery: the incarnation, the passion and the resurrection. The Christian is a man of his time, speaking the language of his time, with a sense of reality and of effective action, though without making pragmatism his leading principle; in short, his wish is to be in touch with the world in order to give God to it. In his wish to consecrate all that is good in the world, he can combine clarity of vision with being open and receptive, and does not show himself systematically opposed to anything just because it is new. In his religious life there must be times of prayer—though not in order to cut him off from his brothers—and other times when he wants to be with others, to proclaim the word of God and celebrate the eucharist. Risen with Christ by baptism, he lives in communion with him, and knows that in him he is united to all his brothers: that knowledge results in unfailing hope, patience and joy. Yet his participation in Christ's resurrection is not complete, and he is still in a condition of suffering which gives him a share in the mystery of the cross. As a disciple of Christ who gave his life to save the world, no Christian can think in terms of a life that excludes the cross: "If any man would come after me, let him deny himself and take up his cross daily and follow me." (Lk 9 : 23.)

The cross is no easier to bear because it is a condition of following the Master and the road that leads to the resurrection; there are times when Christ's prayer to his Father to remove the chalice from him will be found on the lips of his disciples too, before finally becoming consent to God's will. They find the strength to suffer not in themselves, but in union with Christ, and in the context of the church each one's cross has the most miraculous spiritual fruitfulness.

These few aspects of the Christian's situation in the world show that it is a difficult condition in which the uncomfortable is the rule, spiritual self-sufficiency nonsense, and God the only support. The whole thing may be summed up as a total engagement and gift of one's person to the service of Christ.

Showing Christians their role in God's plan

The bible invites Christians to such an engagement, for it makes us aware of our place in the history of salvation, and the part we are called upon to play in it. It shows how utterly irreplaceable each of us is, each personally known and called by God, every vocation having its echo in eternity. A contemporary French writer has put it in this way, which seems to me totally in the spirit of revelation: "If you refuse, eternity will lack that likeness to Christ which only you could produce." It explains to those who are baptised, who belong to the church and live in communion with her, that each has his share in her mission in the place marked out for him by the Lord: this is enough to put us on guard against the inertia so contrary to the Christian vocation, and to make us understand that, on the contrary, every destiny, even when humanly speaking most unsuccessful, has an inestimable value, and perhaps great spiritual profit for the church. Christians find in the word of God an orientation for their lives: the new commandment, the beatitudes, the faith that makes it possible to estimate things from a supernatural standpoint, and the impossibility of separating faith and charity either in our knowledge of God or in our lives. The bible also reveals to the Christian that Christ is the source of his life, and that the church is the place in which he lives that life and it grows. And lastly, it helps him to acquire and to keep, in his response to the Lord's call, a sense of God and of his glory.

The Christian attitude to the revelation of salvation

"Whatever was written in former days was written for our instruction, that by steadfastness and by the encouragement of the scriptures, we might have hope." (Rom 15 : 4.)

The bible, in which God reveals his plan for salvation, was written "for our instruction, upon whom the end of the ages has come" (1 Cor 10 : 11): the Christian's first attitude when God speaks is to receive his word. To neglect to know that word, or to know it only superficially would be a sinful omission which God would in no way be obliged to repair by making up for what would amount to our scorn for revelation by giving us extraordinary private illuminations. God has entrusted it to his church, and charged her to transmit it, to interpret it truly and to apply what it says to the men of each generation. Faithful to her mission, the church feeds the faithful upon the word of God. She never "celebrates the holy mysteries of the eucharist without at the same time breaking the bread of God's word".[1] It is in the church and from the church that Christians receive with faith the word of God, and it was with joy that Catholics read this statement from another Christian some years ago: "Holy Scripture is the book of the church and can only be truly understood within the bosom of the people of God."[2]

The bible is a marvellous prayer-book also, and the texts of the liturgy are woven out of scripture passages: Christians should pray with the bible. If we read it with faith, if we meditate on it in order to find God, if we make our own the psalms which are the prayerful expressions of God's plan, if we look up from the prophets, the gospels or the epistles to raise our hearts to God, then we will gradually work out our own genuinely Christian spirituality.

This in turn will express itself in a practice of the divine word, and lead us to enter, through an ever more perfect life of charity, into the fulfilment of God's plan, and thus to penetrate that wisdom hidden from the wise and prudent and revealed to those who are "in tune" with Christ because of the love he communicates to them.

"May Christ dwell in your hearts through faith; that you, being rooted and grounded in love, may have power to comprehend with all the saints what is the breadth and length and

[1] R. Poelman, *La Bible et le prêtre*, Louvain 1951, 169.
[2] R.M.A., in *Réforme*, 2 Feb. 1957.

height and depth, and to know the love of Christ which surpasses knowledge, that you may be filled with all the fullness of God. Now to him who by the power at work within us is able to do far more abundantly than all that we ask or think, to him be glory in the church and in Christ Jesus to all generations, for ever and ever. Amen." (Eph 3 : 17–21.)

Bibliography

Auzou, G., *La parole de Dieu, approches du mystère des saintes écritures*, Paris, 1956.
—— *La tradition biblique, histoire des écrits sacrés du peuple de Dieu*, Paris, 1957.
Bouyer, L., *La Bible et l'Evangile*, Paris, 1951.
Charlier, C., *The Christian Approach to the Bible*, London, 1958.
Daniélou, J., *The Lord of History*, London, 1958.
Dheilly, J., *Le peuple de l'ancienne Alliance*, Paris, 1954.
Dietrich, S. de, *Le dessein de Dieu* (from the series "Actualité protestante"), Neuchâtel, 1951.
Gelin, A., *Key Concepts of the Old Testament*, London, 1955.
Grelot, P., *Introduction aux Livres Saints*, Paris, 1954.
Grollenberg, L.-H., *Atlas of the Bible*, London, 1957.
Guillet, J., *Thèmes bibliques*, Paris, 1951.
Hasseveldt, R., *Le mystère de l'Eglise*, Paris, 1953.
Imschoot, P. van, *Théologie de l'Ancien Testament*, 2 vols., Paris—Tournai—New York—Rome, vol. 1, 1954; vol. 2, 1956.
Ligue Catholique de l'Evangile, *Cahiers 'Evangile'*, Paris.

LUBAC, H. DE, *The Splendour of the Church*, London, 1956.

ROBERT, A., and FEUILLET, A., *Introduction à la Bible*, Tournai, 1957.

ROBERT, A., and TRICOT, A., *Initiation biblique*, Paris—Tournai—Rome—New York, 1954.